Smart Bread Machine Recipes

Healthy, Wholegrain & Delicious

Sandra L. Woodruff M.S., R.D., L.D.

Illustrated by Joan Columbus

Sterling Publishing Co., Inc.
New York

Edited by Jeanette Green

Library of Congress Cataloging-in-Publication Data

Woodruff, Sandra L.
   Smart bread machine recipes : healthy, whole grain & delicious /
by Sandra L. Woodruff ; illustrated by Joan Columbus.
      p.   cm.
   Includes index.
   ISBN 0-8069-0690-1
   1. Bread.   2. Automatic bread machines.   3. Low-fat diet—Recipes.
I. Title.
TX769.W76   1994
641.8'15—dc20   94-27252
                                                            CIP

1 3 5 7 9 10 8 6 4 2

Published by Sterling Publishing Company, Inc.
387 Park Avenue South, New York, N.Y. 10016
© 1994 by Sandra L. Woodruff
Distributed in Canada by Sterling Publishing
% Canadian Manda Group, One Atlantic Avenue, Suite 105
Toronto, Ontario, Canada M6K 3E7
Distributed in Great Britain and Europe by Cassell PLC
Villiers House, 41/47 Strand, London WC2N 5JE, England
Distributed in Australia by Capricorn Link (Australia) Pty Ltd.
P.O. Box 6651, Baulkham Hills, Business Centre, NSW 2153, Australia
Manufactured in the United States of America
All rights reserved

Sterling ISBN 0-8069-0690-1

Contents

◆ ◆ ◆

Smart Bread Basics

I F YOU LOVE homemade bread, but not the hours spent mixing, kneading, waiting, and cleaning up, an automatic bread-making machine is a dream come true. Many brands are available, but they all function similarly. You simply measure the ingredients, place them in the machine's bread pan, push a button, and come back in a few hours for fresh, hot, homemade bread. Since the machine mixes, kneads, and even bakes the bread in one pan, there is no big mess to clean up. Machines can even be programmed to have freshly baked bread ready when you wake up in the morning.

The real beauty of bread machines, however, is that you can control what goes into your bread. Breads made from wholesome whole grains, with less salt, less fat, and without refined sugar can be yours with the push of a button. This is what *Smart Bread Machine Recipes* is all about. This book presents a tempting assortment of loaves, rolls, sweet breads, pizzas, and other treats made only from the finest, most healthful ingredients.

The Staff of Life

In recent years, bread has reclaimed its status as a healthful food. For decades, bread was shunned by dieters who believed it to be fattening. The fact is, bread is not fattening and never has been. What people put on bread or between bread can be a problem, however. Compare the calories and fat in a slice of bread with what typically goes on top or between.

	Calories	Fat (Grams)
1 slice bread (1 ounce)	70	1
1 tablespoon butter/margarine	100	11
2 tablespoons cream cheese	100	10
1 tablespoon mayonnaise	100	10
1 slice whole milk cheese	100	9
2 ounces luncheon meat	160	16

Fortunately, low-fat spreads and sandwich fillings are widely available today and more people are beginning to choose them. Bread has always been low in fat. Rich in complex carbohydrates and B vitamins, bread fits well into today's dietary recommendations.

Grain products, including whole-grain breads, are the mainstays of fiber-rich, low-fat diets. These foods form the basis of the USDA Food Pyramid Guide and should be included in every meal. It is prudent to eat a minimum of 6 to 11 servings of grain products—including bread, cereal, pasta, and cooked grains every day. The Food Pyramid Guide shows how bread fits into a healthy diet.

White Bread Woes

If bread is good, does that mean white bread too? No. The fact is, white bread contributes to poor health. Sadly, most of the bread people eat today is made from refined white flour, stripped of most of its fiber and nutrients.

How does this affect health? For starters, people who eat refined grain products cannot possibly consume enough fiber for optimal health. They are also likely to have marginal deficiencies of several key nutrients lost during processing. Over time, these deficiencies contribute to diseases like cancer, diabetes, and heart disease.

Food Pyramid Guide

A Guide to Daily Food Choices

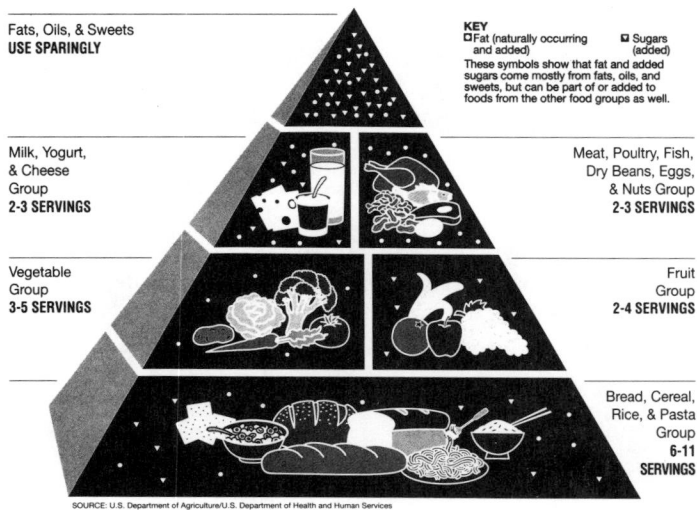

Fats, Oils, & Sweets
USE SPARINGLY

KEY
☐ Fat (naturally occurring and added) ◪ Sugars (added)
These symbols show that fat and added sugars come mostly from fats, oils, and sweets, but can be part of or added to foods from the other food groups as well.

Milk, Yogurt, & Cheese Group
2-3 SERVINGS

Meat, Poultry, Fish, Dry Beans, Eggs, & Nuts Group
2-3 SERVINGS

Vegetable Group
3-5 SERVINGS

Fruit Group
2-4 SERVINGS

Bread, Cereal, Rice, & Pasta Group
6-11 SERVINGS

SOURCE: U.S. Department of Agriculture/U.S. Department of Health and Human Services

Filling with Fiber

Most people eat only half the fiber they need for optimal health. What's so special about fiber? Fiber offers protection against a wide range of health problems: heart disease, diabetes, obesity, constipation, colon cancer, and diverticulosis are just a few of the problems fiber helps prevent. Getting enough fiber is one of the best things you can do for your body.

What Is Fiber?

Dietary fiber, formerly known as old-fashioned roughage, is a type of complex carbohydrate found in *unrefined* plant foods like whole grains, whole-grain flours, fruits, vegetables, and legumes (dried beans). Located in the cell walls of plants, fibers are what give plants their basic structures. Humans (unlike termites) cannot digest fiber; so, it passes through the body largely unchanged. Does this mean fiber has little effect on the body? No. As fiber makes its way through the body, it has a tremendous impact.

Insoluble and Soluble Fiber

There are two kinds of dietary fiber: *insoluble* and *soluble*. Both kinds offer unique health benefits. Insoluble fiber promotes the health and function of the colon (large intestine). In the intestines, insoluble fiber acts like a sponge, absorbing water and keeping the intestinal contents soft—thereby preventing constipation and diverticulosis. Insoluble fiber also pushes wastes and carcinogens quickly through the colon, keeping it clean and disease-free.

Soluble fiber does not have much effect on the colon, but it helps reduce blood cholesterol levels by binding with *bile acids* (raw materials from which cholesterol is made). As bile acids are swept from the body along with soluble fiber, there is less material for making cholesterol. So blood cholesterol concentrations drop. Soluble fiber also helps regulate blood sugar levels by delaying the rise in blood sugar after a meal—this decreases the need for insulin. And it is especially important for people with diabetes.

Fiber Content of Selected Flours

Flour 4 ounces (about 1 cup)	Fiber (grams)
Amaranth	7.6
Barley	13.6
Brown rice	6.0
Buckwheat	14.0
Cornmeal (whole-grain)	9.6
Kamut	8.0
Millet	7.6
Oat	16.0
Rye	15.2
Spelt	10.4
Teff	16.0
Wheat (refined, white)	2.8
White whole wheat flour	13.6
Whole wheat flour	13.6

Watching your weight? All kinds of fiber are slowly absorbed; so, you will feel fuller and more satisfied after a high-fiber meal than after a low-fiber meal. The fact that fibrous foods require more chewing and take longer to eat also makes them more satisfying.

Made properly, bread is an excellent source of fiber. Whole grains contain a mixture of both kinds of fiber; most of the fiber in grains is in the bran (outer layer). Wheat bran is loaded with insoluble fiber. Oats, oat bran, rye, and barley are especially rich in soluble fiber.

How Much Is Enough?

Health experts recommend 25 to 35 grams of dietary fiber daily. Most people eat only half this much. Because fiber helps stabilize blood-sugar concentrations, people with diabetes and hypoglycemia can benefit from slightly more fiber—up to 40 grams per day is recommended (with an emphasis on soluble fibers like those in rye, oats, and barley). It is best to increase your fiber intake gradually rather than making drastic changes that may cause gastrointestinal upset. Always be sure to drink plenty of water (6 to 8 cups per day) when you increase your fiber intake.

Filling the Nutrient Void

Fiber is not all that is lost when grains are refined. Refining strips grains of virtually all their nutrients—nutrients that we need to prevent disease and promote optimal health. At least 20 nutrients are lost during the refining of grains, but only four (thiamine, riboflavin, niacin, and iron) are put back. Refined grains contain almost none of the vitamin B_6, folate, vitamin E, zinc, copper, magnesium, selenium, or chromium naturally present in whole grains. Compare the nutritional effects of refining grains for yourself.

The Scope of the Problem

When you consider the extent to which most people eat refined grains, the impact of refining becomes more clear. Refined white flour is the main ingredient in most breads, rolls, crackers, muffins, biscuits, pancakes, snack foods, pastas, cakes, cookies, and desserts. In addition, many people begin their day with a bowl of cornflakes or other refined cereal. And do not forget about white rice. These foods are a large part of most people's diets. Consumption of refined grain products like these is one reason that most people's diets fall short of the vitamin B_6, vitamin E, magnesium, and chromium they need.

Nutrient Loss in Refining Whole Grains

Vitamin B$_6$	86%	Magnesium	84%
Folate	65%	Phosphorus	75%
Pantothenic Acid	58%	Potassium	73%
Vitamin E	54%*	Zinc	71%
Calcium	60%	Fiber	75%
Copper	66%		

If refined white flour is bleached, vitamin E losses exceed 80%.

Severe nutrient deficiencies are seldom seen today, but health consequences of getting suboptimal amounts of nutrients over a long period of time can be devastating. Marginal nutrient deficiencies contribute to disabling diseases like heart disease, high blood pressure, cancer, diabetes, and more. The table Benefits of Whole-Grain Nutrition lists some benefits of eating the nutrients whole grains offer.

Incorporating whole grains into your diet is easy and delicious; the recipes in this book allow you to make healthful whole-grain breads with the push of a button. Unlike flimsy, tasteless white bread, whole-grain breads have a rich nutty flavor and a chewy, satisfying texture.

Flour Power

Wholesome Whole-Grain Flours

A wide variety of whole-grain flours are available for bread baking, allowing an infinite variety of taste treats. Where can you find whole-grain flours? Almost all grocery stores carry whole-wheat and rye-flours; some feature a variety of other whole-grain flours as well. Natural food stores usually have the best selection of whole-grain flours. Some natural brands are available in both grocery stores and natural food stores. Some companies manufacture a wide variety of organic whole grains and flours.

Benefits of Whole-Grain Nutrition

Nutrient	Functions
Vitamin B$_6$	Necessary for metabolism of protein and fat and for formation of red blood cells.
	Involved in proper nerve functioning.
Folate (Folic Acid)	Needed to form all new cells in the body.
	Especially important during pregnancy to prevent birth defects.
	Helps protect against heart disease.
	Deficiency causes anemia, diarrhea, depression, and impaired immune function.
Vitamin E	Acts as an antioxidant to detoxify destructive free radicals that promote heart disease, cancer, and aging.
	Protects against environmental toxins that exert their effects through free radicals.
	Helps prevent the formation of deadly blood clots.
Chromium	Works with insulin to move sugar from the blood into cells to be used for energy.
	Also involved in fat metabolism.
	Deficiency can result in elevated blood-sugar concentrations and increased levels of fat and cholesterol in the blood.
	An estimated 90% of Americans consume less than the minimum suggested daily amount of chromium.

Nutrient	Functions
Copper	Animal studies show that copper deficiency causes degeneration of the heart and hardening of the arteries.
	Most Americans consume only 75% of the suggested daily amount of copper, a factor that may contribute considerably to heart disease.
Magnesium	Essential for a healthy heart and blood vessels.
	Deficiency causes changes in artery walls that makes them constrict, increasing blood pressure.
	An activator of over 300 enzymes, magnesium is involved in many aspects of metabolism.
Manganese	Necessary for proper nerve functioning, normal bone growth, and blood sugar regulation.
Potassium	Essential for muscle contraction, transmission of nerve impulses, and fluid balance in the body.
	Potassium-rich diets protect against high blood pressure and stroke.
Selenium	As an antioxidant, protects against cancer and other diseases.
Zinc	Essential for proper immune function.
	Helps the body utilize vitamin A.
	Necessary for proper wound healing and sperm synthesis.

Whole-grain flours contain a small amount of vitamin E–rich oil that's naturally present in the whole grain. Because of this, they turn rancid if stored improperly. Should this happen, the flour will exhibit a slightly bitter taste and off-odor instead of its usual slightly sweet, nutty taste and smell. Store whole-grain flours in airtight containers in your pantry for up to six weeks. Even better, store them in the refrigerator or freezer; this greatly increases their shelf life.

When making yeast breads, it is important to realize that flours with the most gluten (a protein that forms the bread's structure) produce the best results. Of all grains, wheat is highest in gluten; this is why it is so widely used in breads. For this reason, wheat flour should form the basis of the bread with other grains substituted for one-fourth to one-third of the wheat flour.

Amaranth (Am' ah ranth)   This tiny, golden-color grain is actually the seed of a native South American plant. Amaranth has an earthy, woody taste and smells like fresh corn silk. One of the most nutritious grains available, amaranth provides significant amounts of calcium, iron, and high-quality protein. Amaranth flour may be substituted for up to one-fourth of the wheat flour in breads. Cooked amaranth can be incorporated into bread doughs as part of the liquid.

Barley   Rich in soluble fiber, barley helps reduce blood cholesterol and stabilizes blood-sugar levels. Barley flour is slightly sweet and adds a tender, cake-like texture to breads. For this reason, it is especially delicious in sweet rolls and dessert breads. Substitute barley flour for up to one-fourth of the wheat flour in loaf breads or for up to one-third of the wheat flour in rolls and pastry doughs.

Buckwheat   Buckwheat is technically not a grain, but the edible fruit seed of a plant closely related to rhubarb. The whole buckwheat kernel is called a *groat*; roasted buckwheat groats are known as *kasha*. Buckwheat's nutty, earthy flavor has long been savored in pancakes, waffles, and Japanese soba noodles. It is also delicious in breads. Substitute buckwheat flour for up to one-fourth of the wheat flour in bread recipes.

Cornmeal   Not just for cornbread, cornmeal gives pumpernickel and anadama breads their characteristic texture. *Unbolted* cornmeal is the whole-corn kernel ground into meal; *bolted* cornmeal is nearly whole grain. *Degermed* cornmeal is refined; so, it contains fewer nutrients and fiber than whole-grain versions. Like all whole grains, corn is a good source of several B vitamins, vitamin E, and dietary fiber.

Toasted Garbanzo Bean Flour   Made from ground garbanzo beans (chick-peas), this flour has a mild, nutty flavor and is rich in protein and nutrients. Use up to 15% garbanzo flour in breads to enhance protein quality and nutrition. Mashed garbanzo beans can also be added to bread dough much like mashed potatoes, pumpkin, and bananas can. Their addition helps bread stay moist.

Kamut (Ka moot')   This ancient strain of wheat is rapidly regaining popularity. Kamut kernels are three times the size of wheat berries and have a delicate, buttery flavor and chewy texture.

Kamut flour may be substituted for wheat flour in any recipe. Grown in the dry regions of northern Montana, Kamut tends to be lower in moisture than common wheat so you may need to add a little more liquid to your bread recipes. Try increasing the liquid by 1 tablespoon per cup of Kamut flour substituted for regular whole wheat flour. Some people who are allergic to wheat report Kamut easier to digest. However, people with wheat allergies should consult with their physician or nutritionist before using Kamut.

Millet   A staple in Oriental and African diets, millet is a good source of B vitamins. Millet flour, available in natural food stores, may be substituted for one-fourth of the wheat flour in breads. Cooked millet can also be incorporated into bread doughs as part of the liquid.

Oats   Rich in B vitamins and cholesterol-lowering soluble fiber, oats have a delicate, slightly sweet flavor that's delicious in breads. Like barley flour, oat flour adds a cake-like texture and works especially well in dessert breads and sweet rolls. Substitute oat flour for 25 to 30% of the wheat flour in yeast breads. Oat flour can be purchased in natural food stores or can be made at home by grinding rolled oats in a blender or food processor until fine.

Oat Bran   The outer part of the oat kernel, oat bran contains most of the fiber and significant amounts of protein, B vitamins, and iron. Substitute oat bran for up to one-fourth of the wheat flour in breads to add soluble fiber and nutrients. Cooked oat bran or oatmeal can be incorporated into bread dough as part of the liquid. Cooking the oats before adding to the dough produces a smooth texture while adding uncooked oats creates a coarser texture.

Quinoa (Keen' wa)   One of the most nutritious grains known, quinoa, is rich in iron, magnesium, copper, and vitamin B_6. Quinoa is also one of the best sources of plant protein available. Unlike most plant proteins, quinoa provides all essential amino acids. Quinoa flour can replace up to 15% of the flour in yeast breads. Cooked quinoa can also be incorporated into bread dough as part of the liquid.

Brown Rice Flour   Whole-grain rice ground into flour, brown rice flour has a light, sweet flavor. Substitute brown rice flour for up to one-fourth of the wheat flour in breads for a lighter taste and cornmeal-like texture.

Rice Bran   The outer part of the brown rice kernel, rice bran is exceptionally rich in thiamine, niacin, B_6, vitamin E, iron, phosphorus, and magnesium. Slightly sweet and nutty-tasting, rice bran is a delicious addition to breads and imparts moistness and tenderness.

Rye This mildly nutty-tasting flour can be purchased in most grocery stores. Replace up to one-half of the wheat flour in breads with rye flour for a hearty, moist loaf. Cooked or sprouted rye berries may also be added to bread dough (use the RAISIN BREAD setting) for a nutty, crunchy effect.

Spelt Like kamut, spelt is an ancient strain of wheat that's gaining renewed interest. Spelt seems to be well tolerated by some wheat-sensitive individuals, but people with wheat allergies should consult with their physician or nutritionist before using it.

Spelt makes an exceptional bread flour. It produces a high-rising loaf without the addition of gluten. Spelt breads have a fine grain, soft texture, and slightly milder flavor than breads made from regular whole-wheat flour. Spelt flour can replace regular whole wheat flour in any recipe; substitute 1 cup plus 1 tablespoon of spelt flour for 1 cup of whole wheat flour. When replacing *refined* wheat flour, substitute spelt one-for-one.

Soybean Flour Loaded with protein and nutrients, small amounts of soy flour can improve the quality of yeast breads. Professional bakers have long known that raw soy flour contains enzymes that condition dough, making it rise better. The amount needed for this effect is a mere ½ to 1 teaspoon per cup of wheat flour. Don't get carried away with soy flour. When soy replaces more than 8% of the wheat flour in yeast breads, the bread begins to taste "beany," the crust darkens too much, and the bread does not rise well.

Teff This tiny grain has been a staple in Ethiopia for centuries. A supernutritious grain, teff provides significant amounts of B vitamins, fiber, calcium, and iron. Teff and teff flour are found mainly in natural food stores. Two varieties are available—dark brown and ivory; both are whole grain. Brown teff's flavor is slightly sweet with a hint of chocolate or molasses. Ivory teff is milder tasting. Substitute up to 20% teff flour for wheat flour in breads. Cooked teff may also be added to bread doughs as part of the liquid.

Triticale A cross between wheat and rye, triticale flour is low in gluten compared to wheat. This means triticale flour must be combined with wheat flour for making yeast breads. Like rye and wheat berries, cooked triticale berries and sprouts are delicious in breads.

Wheat Wheat is rich in the protein gluten, which gives structure to yeast breads and enables them to rise well. For the highest-rising breads, wheat flour should comprise at least two-thirds of the total flour. Other kinds of flours can be incorporated into bread dough to varying degrees. A variety of wheat flours and wheat products are available for use in breads.

- **Whole wheat flour** contains less gluten than refined white flour; this is why 100% whole wheat breads tend to be dense. Fortunately, you can purchase gluten separately and add it to whole wheat flour to improve its rising power (see Secrets of High-Rising, Whole-Grain Yeast Breads).

- **White whole wheat flour** is made from hard *white* wheat instead of the hard *red* wheat that regular whole wheat flour comes from. White whole wheat flour includes all the bran, germ, and nutrition of regular whole wheat flour but has a lighter, sweeter flavor because it lacks the bitter phenolic compounds present in hard red wheat. Bread made from white whole wheat flour will resemble bread made from half refined white flour and half regular whole wheat flour. Substitute 1 cup plus 1 tablespoon of white whole wheat flour for 1 cup of regular whole wheat flour in any recipe. White whole wheat flour can be substituted one-for-one for refined wheat flour in any recipe. White whole wheat flour is available in many grocery stores. It is the predominant kind of wheat in some countries.

- **Bread flour** was developed specifically for yeast breads. Made from high-gluten wheat flour, bread flour also contains dough conditioners like ascorbic acid (vitamin C) and diastatic malt powder (made from sprouted barley) which also help bread rise.

  The bread flour commonly available in grocery stores is made from refined wheat flour, but you can make your own using the recipe for Homemade Bread Flour from whole wheat flour or unbleached flour if you like.

Homemade Bread Flour

6 cups	flour (unbleached or whole wheat)
1 tbsp	wheat gluten
1 tbsp	diastatic malt powder
1 tsp	ascorbic acid

- **Whole wheat pastry flour** is a low-protein flour best suited for quick breads, muffins, pastries, and pie crusts. It is not recommended for yeast breads because it does not have enough gluten to provide proper structure for optimal rising. Occasionally you may see a recipe for yeast-raised sweet rolls or pastry items that call for whole wheat pastry flour.

- **Unbleached flour** is refined white flour. Stripped of its germ and bran, unbleached flour lacks fiber and many nutrients compared to whole wheat flour. Unbleached flour is so named because it is not subjected to the chemical bleaching process that whitens bleached flour. Bleaching destroys the small amount of vitamin E that remains in flour after milling. For this reason, unbleached flour is superior to bleached.

- **Whole wheat berries**, available in natural food stores, are the whole-grain wheat kernel. Cooked wheat berries added to bread dough produce a chewy texture and nutty taste (use the RAISIN BREAD setting for adding wheat berries or they will get pulverized during kneading).

- **Cracked wheat** is the wheat berry that has been coarsely ground; add cooked cracked wheat to bread dough as part of the liquid for a hearty flavor and texture.

- **Rolled-wheat flakes** are whole wheat kernels flattened into flakes. Like cracked wheat, cooked rolled wheat can be incorporated into bread dough as part of the liquid.

Secrets of High-Rising, Whole-Grain Yeast Breads

Each brand of bread-maker comes with recipes, but few come with recipes for 100% whole-grain, low-fat, low-salt, breads. Modifying your own recipes for yeast breads can be tricky, especially when using a machine programmed to knead, rise, and bake at specific times. Some tips will help you transform your own favorite bread recipes into more healthful versions.

Adding Fiber

Yeast breads made with white (refined) flour rise better than whole-grain breads because white flour contains more gluten, the protein that gives strength and elasticity to dough. Breads made with 100% whole-grain flours will be very dense unless gluten is added. Fortunately, gluten may be purchased at natural food stores and many grocery stores. Add 1½ teaspoons of gluten for each cup of whole wheat flour used in a recipe. With the addition of gluten to bread doughs, you can replace all the white flour in your bread recipes with whole wheat flour.

Other whole-grain flours such as oatmeal, rye, or barley flour can comprise one-fourth to one-half of the flour in yeast breads. These flours have even less gluten than whole wheat flour; so, add 2 to 3 teaspoons of gluten for each cup of these flours used.

Be sure to use pure wheat gluten, usually referred to as *vital* wheat gluten in your recipes. *Gluten flour,* a mixture of vital wheat gluten and wheat flour, is also available for baking but will not give bread the same boost as vital wheat gluten.

Reducing Fat

Fats such as butter, margarine, and oil are added to breads to produce a soft, moist texture, but perfectly fine breads can be made with little or no fat. When eliminating fat from a yeast-bread recipe, be sure to increase the liquid or the dough will be too stiff.

Most yeast breads do not contain an excessive amount of fat, and fat spread on at the table is usually a bigger problem than the fat that goes into them. The breads in this book contain no more than 1 tablespoon of fat per 1-pound loaf. This is enough to produce a soft texture, enhance rising, and prevent the bread from becoming stale quickly. Ingredients like fruit juices, nonfat buttermilk, and yogurt are frequently included in these recipes to enhance texture and flavor, reducing the need for fat.

Lecithin—A Super Fat

Commercial bread bakers frequently add *lecithin* to yeast breads. Derived from soybean oil, lecithin is an emulsifier—it makes things mix better. Lecithin is highly recommended for bread baking. Why? For the same amount of fat, lecithin conditions the dough much better and produces a softer-textured, higher-rising loaf. Lecithin is available in either liquid or granular form; both forms are available at natural food stores.

How are liquid and granular lecithin different? Lecithin liquid is a very thick, sticky oil—it is almost impossible to work with because it sticks to everything. Lecithin granules are puffed up bits of oil that can be easily measured and used in recipes. Because the granules are puffed, they cannot be substituted for liquids one-for-one. The recipes in this book call for lecithin granules; if you use the liquid form, use half as much because it's more dense. If you prefer, an equal amount of vegetable oil, butter, or margarine can substitute for lecithin granules. Breads made with oil will be slightly denser than those made with lecithin.

Like all fats, lecithin liquid has 120 calories per tablespoon (the granules have half the calories because they are less dense). Unlike most fats though, lecithin is rich in nutrients, especially vitamin E, iron, phosphorus, and choline. Refrigerate lecithin to prevent rancidity.

Slashing Salt

Salt is needed in yeast breads to control the rising of the yeast. Salt-free breads rise too quickly and have a weak texture. However, salt can be reduced by half with no adverse effect. To reduce salt in yeast breads, simultaneously reduce the amount of yeast so the bread does not rise too fast. This is especially important for breads made in automatic bread-makers that knead, rise, and bake at specific times. Doughs that contain too little salt will rise too rapidly, then fall before automatic baking begins. In general, reduce yeast by the same percent that salt is reduced. For example, if you reduce salt by half, reduce the yeast by half too. You may have to experiment with the recipe a few times to get it just right.

The recipes in this book are made with finely ground *sea salt,* but regular table salt will work as well. How is sea salt different from standard table salt? All salt originates from sea water. The main difference between sea salt and commercial grocery store varieties is in the amount of processing. Sea salt tends to be less processed and contains fewer additives.

Most commercial brands of salt contain anticaking agents, crystal modifiers, iodine, and dextrose (sugar). Decades ago, iodine deficiency was a public health problem. Today the reverse is true; iodine is a common additive in many processed foods and some people are consuming too much of it.

Look for sea salt in natural food stores and many grocery stores. Select brands that are *sun-evaporated.* Sea salt often contains magnesium carbonate to prevent caking; this is a safe additive.

Dough Enhancers

Certain ingredients, like gluten and lecithin, enhance the quality of yeast-bread doughs. Two other dough enhancers are *ascorbic acid* (vitamin C) and *diastatic malt powder.* Both are added to commercial bread flour to improve their performance in yeast breads. You may add these ingredients to the recipes in this book, if you like.

The addition of ascorbic acid to dough makes it rise better. This is especially important for sweet breads, which tend to rise very slowly. Ascorbic acid changes the pH of the dough, making it slightly more acidic and, therefore, more hospitable to yeast. To enhance rising, you may add ¼ teaspoon of ascorbic acid powder to the ingredients for a 1½-pound loaf. For a 1-pound loaf, use slightly less (fill a ¼-teaspoon measure two-thirds full). Three teaspoons of lemon juice or vinegar added to a 1½-pound loaf (or 2 teaspoons added to a 1-pound loaf) can substitute for ascorbic acid.

Many breads in this book include ingredients like fruit juice, buttermilk, and yogurt. These slightly acidic beverages have the same conditioning effect on dough that ascorbic acid does. Do not add ascorbic acid to recipes that contain these ingredients. Too much acid slows the growth of yeast.

Diastatic malt powder is made from sprouted barley. This dough conditioner contains enzymes that produce a finer texture, enhance flavor, and retain freshness in yeast breads. Add ½ teaspoon of diastatic malt powder to the ingredients for a 1½-pound loaf. For a 1-pound loaf, use ⅓ teaspoon (fill a ½ teaspoon measure two-thirds full).

Look for ascorbic acid and diastatic malt in specialty stores and natural food stores.

Sweeter Options
Using Sweeteners in Yeast Breads

Yeast breads can be made without any sugar at all, but when a little sugar is included in the recipe it activates the yeast better. Most yeast breads do not contain enough sugar to worry about. Sweeteners like honey, molasses, Sucanat, and barley malt add flavor, texture, and color to bread. Most breads in this book contain 1 to 2 tablespoons of sweetener per loaf, just enough to add flavor, enhance browning, and produce a tender texture. Here are some wholesome sweeteners available.

Liquid Sweeteners

These liquid sweeteners add both sweetness and moisture to yeast breads. If you substitute a liquid sweetener for sugar, reduce liquid elsewhere in the recipe to compensate, or the dough will be too moist.

Amazake (Ah mah za' kay)   A sweetener made from fermented brown rice (fermentation transforms rice starches into sugars). Pure amazake is thick, creamy, and mildly sweet. Amazake sweetens many rice-based puddings, frozen desserts, and beverages sold in natural food stores. Use amazake in breads as you would honey or any other liquid sweetener. Amazake is not as sweet as honey; so, you may want to use a bit more.

Amazake-Rice Beverage   This is a creamy drink made from amazake, water, and flavorings. Fresh amazake beverages can be found in the refrigerator section of natural food stores. Shelf-stable, aseptically packaged beverages are also available; choose from traditional and light versions. Use amazake beverages for all or part of the liquid in yeast breads to eliminate need for sugar. One cup of beverage has sweetness equal to 3 to 4 tablespoons of sugar (light varieties are less sweet).

Barley-Malt Syrup   Available in natural food stores, barley-malt syrup is extracted from sprouted barley. It looks similar to molasses and has a distinctive malt taste that adds a delicious dimension to whole-grain breads. Barley malt is about one-third as sweet as sugar. Be sure to buy pure barley-malt syrup, not the bitter hop-flavored kind used for making beer.

Brown Rice Syrup   This is made in a process similar to that of corn syrup except the whole grain, only slightly polished, is used. (Refined starch is used in making corn syrup.) Brown rice syrup retains most of the nutrients in brown rice and has a delicate malted flavor that's delicious in breads. Depending on the brand, brown-rice syrup is 30 to 60% as sweet as sugar.

Fruitsource   Fruitsource is a liquid sweetener made from grape juice concentrate and brown rice syrup. It has a rather neutral flavor and is as sweet as sugar. Use it as you would honey or molasses.

Fruits   Fruit purees, applesauce, mashed bananas, and fruit juices can all be used in breads instead of sugar. The natural sugars in fruits feed the yeast, eliminating the need for other added sugars. Incorporate fruits and fruit purees as part of the liquid; 1/2-cup of pureed fruit or fruit juice contains 1 to 2 tablespoons of sugar, enough for a 1-pound loaf. Try a little of apple or prune juice in rye bread, mashed banana in whole wheat bread, and pear nectar or orange juice in raisin bread.

Honey   Contrary to popular belief, honey is not significantly more nutritious than sugar, but it does add a nice flavor to breads, especially whole-grain breads. Many varieties of honey are available, each with its own distinct flavor. Honey is about 20% sweeter than sugar.

Molasses   This flavorful sweetener adds rich flavor and a dark color to breads. It's especially delicious in rye breads. Of all sweeteners, only molasses provides significant amounts of nutrients, including potassium, calcium, and iron. Light molasses, the kind commonly used for baking, is widely available in grocery stores. Be sure to buy unsulfured molasses to avoid added sulfites that many people are sensitive to. **Blackstrap molasses**, a concentrated byproduct of sugar-making, is especially rich in nutrients. Do not add more than 1 or 2 tablespoons of blackstrap per loaf though—its bitter taste will overwhelm the bread.

Sugar Cane Syrup   The boiled juice extracted from sugar canes, cane syrup adds flavor as well as potassium to breads. Use it as you would honey or molasses.

Maple Syrup   The boiled-down sap of maple trees, maple syrup adds delicious flavor to breads. Maple syrup provides some potassium and other nutrients. Use it as you would honey or molasses; it is about 60% as sweet.

Sorghum Molasses   Sorghum molasses is the boiled-down juice of the sorghum plant, a grain. Nutritionally comparable to light molasses, sorghum has a tart, fruity molasses-like flavor that enhances the flavors of whole-grain breads.

Granulated Sweeteners

These granulated sweeteners are better choices than white sugar because they are less refined and more wholesome. These sweeteners may be used interchangeably in any recipes in this book that call for sugar.

Date Sugar   Made from ground, dried dates, this coarsely ground sweetener provides potassium, copper, magnesium, iron, and B vitamins. Date sugar is slightly less sweet than white sugar but has more flavor.

Fruitsource   Fruitsource contains granules of dehydrated grape juice and brown-rice syrup, Fruitsource is available in natural food stores. Fruitsource has a mild flavor and is 80% as sweet as sugar.

Maple Sugar   Maple syrup dehydrated into granules, maple sugar is delicious substituted for sugar in breads. Powdered maple sugar may also be used in glazes instead of powdered confectioner's sugar.

Sucanat   Sugar created the way nature intended, Sucanat is granules of evaporated sugar cane juice. Sucanat provides small amounts of potassium, chromium, calcium, iron, and vitamins A and C. Sucanat tastes similar to brown sugar.

Using Dairy Products in Breads

Dairy products, like skim milk, nonfat buttermilk, nonfat yogurt, and cottage cheese, add protein, calcium, and other nutrients to breads while enhancing flavor and texture. Here are some tips for using these ingredients.

Skim Milk   Milk adds a rich texture and flavor to breads. Unfortunately, some of the proteins in milk weaken gluten, adversely affecting bread quality. This problem is easily overcome by scalding milk before adding it to bread dough, because heat inactivates proteins. Milk used in yeast breads that don't depend on strong gluten development for structure does not need to be scalded. Examples are pizza crusts, flat breads, soft pretzels, and sweet rolls.

Nonfat Buttermilk and Yogurt   These cultured milk products are interchangeable in recipes. Both add flavor and produce a moist, rich texture in breads. Unlike milk, buttermilk or yogurt does not need to be heated before being added to bread doughs. Buttermilk and yogurt can replace part or all of the liquid in most bread recipes.

You will need slightly more buttermilk or yogurt than water or skim milk to hydrate the same amount of flour. Watch the dough as it kneads and add more buttermilk or yogurt, 1 tablespoon at a time, until the dough reaches the proper consistency.

Nonfat and Low-Fat Cottage Cheese   Cottage cheese imparts moisture and a light, airy texture to breads. It makes especially good rolls. For each ½ cup of cottage cheese added to a yeast-bread recipe, reduce water or another liquid by about 6 tablespoons. Cottage-cheese breads tend to rise quickly; so, you may need to reduce the yeast a bit for breads baked inside the machine. Otherwise, the bread may rise prematurely, then fall before automatic baking begins. For example, if a recipe calls for 1 teaspoon of yeast, try ¾ teaspoon.

Vegetarian Alternatives   People who do not use dairy products have a variety of nondairy alternatives to choose from. Here are some examples.

- **Soy milk** and **soy yogurt** are available in natural food stores and many grocery stores; they can be used instead of their dairy counterparts in any yeast-bread recipe. Soy milk actually improves the quality of bread doughs and imparts a tender texture. Unlike dairy milk, soy milk does not have to be scalded before being added to bread dough.

  You can even make a soy alternative to **buttermilk**—put 1 tablespoon of vinegar in a 1-cup measure; add soy milk to the 1-cup mark. Stir and let sit for 5 minutes. This makes 1 cup of soy buttermilk. Soy buttermilk will be slightly thinner than dairy buttermilk; so, you may need to use a little less to moisten a given amount of flour. Try substituting ⅞ cup of soy buttermilk for 1 cup of dairy buttermilk.

- **Almond milk**, slightly sweet and nutty, can be easily made at home in a blender. Grind ¼ cup of blanched almonds in a blender until fine. Add 2 cups of water and continue to blend until creamy; shake before using. This makes 2 cups. Almond milk contains 8 grams of fat per cup (the same as whole cow's milk), but the fat is unsaturated and comes packaged with vitamin E and other nutrients. Macadamia nuts, Brazil nuts, cashews, and sunflower seeds also make delicious milks. Nut milks contain small amounts of calcium (30 to 45 mg per cup).

- **Rice beverages**, made from brown rice, are light and refreshing. They are available plain or flavored, in regular and low-fat varieties. Unless they are fortified, rice beverages are not a significant source of calcium. Use plain, unflavored rice beverages as you would dairy milk; they do not require scalding before being added to bread dough.

  Flavored rice beverages are sweeter than the plain versions. When using flavored rice beverages in bread dough, reduce the sugar accordingly. Depending on the brand, 1 cup of flavored rice beverage has sweetness equal to 1½ to 3 tablespoons of sugar.

Basic Tips for Best-Ever Yeast Breads

Here's a summary of the most important aspects of baking whole-grain, low-fat breads in a bread machine. Paying close attention to these tips will assure successful bread baking.

- When substituting whole wheat flour for refined, add 1½ teaspoons of wheat gluten for each cup of whole wheat flour that replaces the refined flour. Add 2 to 3 teaspoons of gluten per cup of other whole-grain flours, like oat, barley, and rye. This makes the bread rise higher.

- When reducing salt in a yeast-bread machine recipe, decrease the amount of yeast proportionately. Otherwise, the bread will rise too quickly and adversely affect texture.

- For a softer texture and better rising, use lecithin instead of oil or margarine. One tablespoon of granules is generally sufficient for 1-pound loaf.

- Try adding ½ teaspoon of diastatic malt powder to the ingredients for a 1½-pound loaf (use two-thirds as much for a 1-pound loaf). Enzymes in diastatic malt powder condition dough, making it rise better and improving texture.

- Try adding ¼ teaspoon of ascorbic acid to ingredients for a 1½-pound loaf (use two-thirds as much for a 1-pound loaf). This changes the pH of the dough and improves rising. Do not add ascorbic acid to recipes that already contain acidic ingredients like fruit juice, applesauce, buttermilk, yogurt, and lemon juice.

- Check the dough for proper hydration after it kneads for several minutes. The dough should form a smooth satiny ball, not a sticky mess. If dough is sticking to the sides of the pan, add more flour 1 tablespoon at a time. If the dough has formed a tight, stiff ball, add more liquid, ½ tablespoon at a time until it reaches the proper consistency. Too much liquid will make the loaf porous and weak-textured. Too little liquid will prevent the bread from rising optimally.

- Use only fresh yeast. Check the expiration date; do not use yeast past this date. Refrigerate yeast to maintain freshness. Use regular active dry yeast or rapid-rise yeast; both work equally well in the recipes in this book.

- Add raisins, chopped fruits, nuts, and seeds near the end of the first kneading cycle. Most machines have a RAISIN BREAD, MIX BREAD, or similar setting that lets you know when to add ingredients like these. Added too early, they will become pulverized beyond recognition.

Sprouted Breads

Spruce up breads with sprouted grains. Wheat berries, rye berries, and triticale can all be sprouted and added to bread dough. Slightly sweet and chewy, sprouts are rich in B vitamins, minerals, and fiber. To get started, all you need is a 1-quart widemouthed glass jar, a specially designed lid with small holes or screening (found at any natural food store), and your chosen grain.

Sprouted grains contain *diastatic* enzymes (the same enzymes found in diastatic malt powder) that improve the quality of bread dough, enabling it to rise better. They also contain a sugar called maltose that adds a distinctive malt flavor to breads. Wheat sprouts are especially flavorful in yeast breads. Use about ½ cup of whole wheat sprouts per 1-pound loaf of bread (use the RAISIN BREAD setting when adding sprouts or they'll be pulverized). A word of caution—the grains on the outside will be crunchy; so, chew carefully.

For a cracked-wheat effect, add chopped wheat sprouts to bread dough. Chopping sprouts releases more enzymes that condition dough; so, be careful since too many enzymes make the bread a gooey mess. Use 3 to 4 tablespoons of chopped sprouts per loaf of bread for optimal results. In breads where you want the conditioning effect of wheat sprouts without wheat-berry or cracked-wheat particles, puree 1½ tablespoons of wheat sprouts with the liquid for the bread before mixing with flour.

Sprouts can cause bread to rise unpredictably. So, your safest bet is to let your machine mix and raise the dough once; then, shape it yourself and bake it in the oven. Make a braided loaf, a hearty round loaf, rolls, or even pizza crust with added sprouts.

Sprouting Made Simple

Here are basic directions for sprouting grains. Any kind of grain can be sprouted. Wheat berries and rye berries are two of the easiest and tastiest.

- Cover the bottom of a widemouthed glass jar with your chosen grain. Do not put too much grain in the jar.

- Seal the jar with a sprouting lid (a specially designed lid with screening or holes in it). Cover the grain with water, and let it soak in a dark place overnight.

- The next day, drain the grains and rinse with fresh, cool water. Lay the jar on its side and put it in a dark place.

- Rinse with cool water twice daily and drain well until the sprout is as long as the grain. Sprouts that grow too long tend to make breads gummy and dense.

- The sprouts will be ready in 2 to 3 days. When they are long enough, rinse and dry off, then use them immediately or refrigerate them until they're ready to use. Sprouts will keep in the refrigerator for 2 to 3 days.

Helpful Hints

Before You Begin Bread-Making

Dealing with Different Sizes of Machines

The recipes in this book can be used with automatic bread-makers that produce 1-pound, 1½-pound, and 2-pound loaves. For breads baked *inside* the machine, ingredient amounts are given for both 1-pound and 1½-pound models. If you have a 2-pound machine, simply double ingredients given for the 1-pound loaf. How do you know what size machine you have? One-pound loaf machines generally call for about 2 cups of flour per loaf of bread, 1½-pound loaves require about 3 cups of flour, and 2-pound loaves require about 4 cups of flour.

Conversions are important for breads baked in the machine. For coffee cakes, rolls, pizzas, and loaves baked outside the machine, follow the standard recipe unless you want a larger quantity than the recipe allows.

Using the Delay Timer

When using the bread machine's delay timer, be sure to keep the yeast away from liquid ingredients. Yeast must remain dry until mixing time; otherwise, it will begin to ferment and lose its potency. To assure that the yeast stays dry when using the delay timer, put liquid ingredients in the pan first, followed by the flour, salt, sugar, and any other dry ingredients. Sprinkle the yeast over the top of the dry ingredients.

Note: Do not use the delay timer for breads containing eggs or dairy products. Left in the pan too long, these ingredients will spoil.

Machine Settings

Most machines have a variety of settings like these.

RAISIN BREAD This setting may also be called **MIX BREAD** or **FRUIT & NUT**. This is the setting you need when making breads that contain raisins, chopped dried fruit, nuts, or seeds. At this setting, the machine beeps about 12 minutes after kneading starts. This tells you to add the fruits, nuts, or seeds. Added too early, ingredients like these become pulverized beyond recognition.

Some models do not have a special setting for adding ingredients; instead they automatically beep or buzz when it is time to add ingredients.

RISE   This is also called a DOUGH or MANUAL setting. Use this setting when you want to make rolls, breadsticks, pizza crust, bagels, or any shaped bread other than the standard loaf that bakes in the machine. This setting mixes, kneads, and allows dough to rise once. When these steps are completed, the machine beeps. At this time, remove the dough, shape it as desired, and allow it to rise once more before baking.

CRUST COLOR   This setting allows you to choose a light, medium, or dark crust by varying oven temperature or baking time slightly. The higher the oven temperature and the longer the baking time, the darker the crust will be. A word of warning: if you discover that your bread is not getting done in the middle, check your CRUST COLOR setting. At the lightest setting, some breads may fail to cook all the way through.

SWEET   Sweet breads and dessert breads, which have a higher sugar content than other breads, tend to brown more easily and rise more slowly. Some machines have a special setting for sweet breads, which may include a longer rising time and lower baking temperature. If your machine does not have this setting, use the light CRUST COLOR setting for sweet loaves.

WHOLE WHEAT   This setting, featured on some brands of machines, offers more power and is designed to efficiently knead whole-grain flours which are heavier than refined flours. It may also include a longer rising time. If your machine has a WHOLE WHEAT setting, use it for bread recipes in this book. However, these doughs were developed to work in any machine.

Measuring Ingredients

Measure ingredients carefully and correctly. The right proportion of liquid to flour assures the dough is not too stiff or too soft. Use dry measuring cups for dry ingredients and liquid measuring cups for liquid ingredients.

The right proportion of yeast to salt assures that the bread does not rise too quickly or too slowly. Use measuring spoons for these ingredients.

Temperature of Liquids

Unlike conventional yeast-bread recipes, you don't have to preheat liquids before adding them to these recipes. Liquids, like yogurt and buttermilk, should be warmed to room temperature before adding them to the bread pan. Water can be used straight from the tap.

Baking at High Altitudes

These recipes were developed at sea level. Breads rise faster at high altitudes; so, you may need to make minor changes in the recipes. How will you know if this is a problem for you? If your bread is rising so fast that its texture is coarse and holey or the top collapses before automatic baking begins, you need to make adjustments. To rectify the problem, try using less yeast. Begin with a 10% reduction if the bread has a coarse, holey texture near the top. Try a 25% reduction if the bread collapses before the baking cycle begins. Your owner's manual or the local extension office of the maker of your bread machine may be able to provide more information.

You can also slow down rising by adding a little more salt. The recipes in this book use about half the salt of traditional recipes. So, even if you add a little more salt, the breads will still have less sodium than most breads. Try increasing the salt by 10 to 25% as an alternative to reducing the yeast. Air tends to be drier at high altitudes, so you may need to add an additional 1 to 2 tablespoons of liquid to the recipe.

Nutrition Analysis

Nutrition analysis is provided for all recipes. These values were determined by computer using the Food Processor II Nutrition and Diet Analysis System (© 1988, ESHA Research).

Where you have a choice of ingredients, nutrition analysis is based on the first ingredient listed. For example, if a recipe allows the option of using nonfat or reduced-fat cheese, analysis has been calculated using nonfat cheese. The nutrition analysis is listed *per serving*. One serving would be, for example, one slice of bread, one roll, one bagel, or one slice of pizza.

Problem Solving

Having problems? Measurement errors, omitting ingredients, and variations in ambient temperature and humidity can all affect bread.

Slight variations in the way different brands of machines work can also affect outcome and may require small adjustments in recipes. For example, if you find

Bread Machine Problems and Possible Causes

Problem	Possible Causes
Poor Rising	Forgot to add yeast. Forgot to add gluten. Yeast may be old (check expiration date). Measurement errors—too much salt, not enough yeast. Dough too stiff—not enough liquid. Delay timer was used and ingredients were placed in the pan in such a manner that the yeast contacted the liquid and activated too early. If poor rising is a consistent problem, try increasing the yeast; start with ¼ teaspoon.
Undercooked Loaf	Too much liquid in recipe. Crust color setting too light—oven temperature may be too low.
Soggy Crust	Bread left in pan too long after baking completed.
Uneven Top	Too little liquid can cause a lopsided loaf by making the dough too stiff to spread evenly.
Collapsed Top	Too much liquid. Too much yeast—the bread will rise then fall before the baking cycle beings. Not enough salt—this will also make bread rise so quickly that it falls before the baking cycle begins. Altitude may be a problem. Breads tend to rise faster at high altitudes. If a collapsed top is a consistent problem, try reducing the yeast; start with ¼ teaspoon.

Problem	Possible Causes
Coarse or Holey Texture	Too much liquid. Liquids added were too warm and hastened fermentation of yeast—use room temperature liquids only. Too much yeast. Forgot salt. Altitude may be a problem. Breads tend to rise faster at high altitudes.
Height or Shape of Loaves from the Same Recipe Differ	Variations in ambient temperature or humidity. Errors when measuring ingredients.
Flour on the Loaf's Sides	Some flour stuck to the side of the machine during kneading. Use a rubber spatula to push flour off sides of pan during kneading cycle.
Burning Smell During Baking	Flour may have splashed over the sides of the pan during kneading onto the heating element. Do not overload machine.
Kneading Bar Embedded in Loaf	Use a wooden spoon or rubber spatula to remove it. Be careful not to scratch the bar.
Crust Too Dark	Try a lighter CRUST-COLOR setting. If your machine doesn't have this feature, remove the loaf a few minutes before baking is normally complete. Turn the machine off and use pot holders to remove the bread pan. Turn the loaf onto a rack to cool. If a loaf comes out a bit underdone, all is not lost; it will make fine toast.

that your bread is consistently coming out too compact, you might find that increasing the yeast by ¼ teaspoon produces optimal results in your machine.

Here's a list of common bread-machine pitfalls and problem-solving strategies. Paying close attention to measuring and getting a feel for proper dough consistency will eliminate most problems.

Slicing & Storing Bread

Unlike flimsy white breads, firmly textured whole-grain breads can be sliced warm. However, if you plan to keep the bread a few days, it's best to allow the bread to cool before slicing. Slicing bread while it's still warm allows moisture to escape; and so, leftovers become dry and stale more quickly.

Use a bread knife for slicing bread. A bread knife has a long blade with a very sharp, serrated edge. Slice bread with a light hand, using a gentle sawing motion. Avoid using too much downward pressure or you will smash the bread.

Bread is best stored at room temperature. Breads like those in this book (made without preservatives) remain fresh for about two days at room temperature. Avoid storing bread in the refrigerator, since it will become hard and stale quickly. If you want to keep leftover bread, wrap it tightly and freeze it.

Hearty, Whole-Grain Loaves

T HESE HEARTY LOAVES, made with a variety of whole grains and flours, are all easily baked inside the machine. Some of these breads are made with raisins, nuts, or seeds; use the RAISIN BREAD, MIX BREAD, or equivalent setting as directed. Some machines do not have a special setting for adding nuts or fruits. Instead, they automatically beep to let you know when to add these ingredients. See your instruction manual for more information. Ingredient amounts are given for both 1-pound and 1½-pound loaves.

Baking the Perfect Loaf

For best results, measure ingredients carefully. Scoop flour into a dry measuring cup, and level off the top with the flat end of a knife or spatula. Use a glass measuring cup for liquid ingredients. Use measuring spoons for yeast, salt, lecithin, gluten, and other minor ingredients.

Warm or hot liquids should never be used in these recipes. Use room-temperature water straight from the tap. Liquids, like buttermilk, yogurt, and juices, should be warmed to room temperature.

For breads to be made immediately, it really doesn't matter what order the ingredients are placed in the pan. If you are using the delay timer, put the liquid ingredients on the bottom and the dry ingredients on top, taking care to keep the yeast dry. Never use the delay timer for recipes that contain perishable ingredients.

Be sure to read the Helpful Hints in the "Smart Bread Basics" chapter before you begin.

Using Lecithin

Lecithin is the ideal oil for low-fat yeast breads. For the same amount of fat, lecithin conditions the dough better and produces a loaf with softer texture that's higher rising. Lecithin is available in either liquid or granular form; both kinds are available in natural food stores. These recipes call for lecithin granules. If you choose to use liquid lecithin, use half as much, because it's more dense. If you use vegetable oil instead of lecithin, use 1 tablespoon of oil as a substitute for 1 tablespoon of lecithin granules.

Whole Wheat–Buttermilk Bread

	1-pound	1½-pound
whole wheat flour	2 cups	3 cups
wheat gluten	1 tbsp	1½ tbsp
sea salt	½ tsp	¾ tsp
yeast	1 tsp	1½ tsp
sugar	1 tbsp	1½ tbsp
lecithin granules or vegetable oil	1 tbsp	1½ tbsp
nonfat buttermilk	1 cup	1½ cups

Put everything in the machine's bread pan and turn the machine on. A 1-pound loaf makes 12 (1.45 ounce) slices, and a 1½-pound loaf makes 18 slices.

Buttermilk produces yeast bread with a rich taste and soft texture while adding calcium, potassium, and protein.

PER SERVING ───────────────────────

| Calories: 87 | Sodium: 110 mg | Cholesterol: 0 mg |
| Fat: 1.1 g | Protein: 3.7 g | Fiber: 2.5 g |

Honey Whole Wheat Bread

	1-pound	1½-pound
whole wheat flour	2 cups	3 cups
wheat gluten	1 tbsp	1½ tbsp
yeast	¾ tsp	1⅛ tsp
sea salt	½ tsp	¾ tsp
honey	2 tbsp	3 tbsp
lecithin granules or vegetable oil	1 tbsp	1½ tbsp
water	¾ cup + 1 tbsp	1¼ cup

Put everything in the machine's bread pan and turn the machine on. A 1-pound loaf makes 12 (1.45 ounce) slices, and a 1½-pound loaf makes 18 slices.

PER SERVING

Calories: 86	Sodium: 90 mg	Cholesterol: 0 mg
Fat: 0.9 g	Protein: 3 g	Fiber: 2.5g

Variations

Cinnamon-Raisin Bread   Add ¾ teaspoon of cinnamon along with the dry ingredients. Use the RAISIN BREAD setting, and add ½ cup of raisins when the machine beeps. Use 1⅛ tsp of cinnamon and ¾ cup of raisins for a 1½-pound loaf.

Three-Seed Bread   Use the RAISIN BREAD setting, and add 1 tablespoon each of sunflower, sesame, and flax seeds. Use 1½ tablespoons of each for a 1½-pound loaf.

Applesauce Oat Bread

Sweetened naturally with applesauce, this loaf makes a delicious sandwich bread. Because oats taste milder than whole wheat, this is a good beginning bread for people not accustomed to 100% whole-grain breads.

	1-pound	1½-pound
whole wheat flour	1½ cups	2¼ cups
oat flour	½ cup	¾ cup
wheat gluten	1½ tbsp	2¼ tbsp
yeast	1 tsp	1½ tsp
sea salt	½ tsp	¾ tsp
lecithin granules or vegetable oil	1 tbsp	1½ tbsp
unsweetened applesauce	1 cup	1½ cups

Put everything in the machine's bread pan and turn the machine on. A 1-pound loaf makes 12 (1.4 ounce) slices, and a 1½-pound loaf makes 18 slices.

PER SERVING ————————————————————————————

Calories: 88	Sodium: 90 mg	Cholesterol: 0 mg
Fat: 1.1 g	Protein: 3.3 g	Fiber: 2.7 g

Variations

Applesauce Date Nut Bread   Use the RAISIN BREAD setting, and add ⅓ cup of chopped dried dates and ¼ cup of chopped walnuts when the machine beeps. Use ½ cup of dates and ⅓ cup of nuts for a 1½-pound loaf.

Applesauce Raisin Bread   Use the RAISIN BREAD setting, and add ½ cup of raisins when the machine beeps. Use ¾ cup of raisins for a 1½-pound loaf.

Wheat Berry Bread

Wheat berries add a nutty crunch to this fruit-juice sweetened bread. Chew carefully, wheat berries in the crust can become quite crunchy.

	1-pound	1½-pound
whole wheat flour	2 cups	3 cups
wheat gluten	1 tbsp	1½ tbsp
yeast	1 tsp	1½ tsp
sea salt	½ tsp	¾ tsp
lecithin granules or vegetable oil	1 tbsp	1½ tbsp
white grape juice	¾ cup + 2 tbsp	1¼ cups + 1 tbsp
cooked wheat berries	½ cup	¾ cup

Put everything except wheat berries in the machine's bread pan and turn the machine on to the RAISIN BREAD setting. Add the wheat berries when the machine buzzes. A 1-pound loaf makes 12 (1.6 ounce) slices, and a 1½-pound loaf makes 18 slices.

PER SERVING

Calories: 88	Sodium: 90 mg	Cholesterol: 0 mg
Fat: 0.9 g	Protein: 3.2 g	Fiber: 2.8 g

Getting Used to Grains

Not accustomed to the hearty taste and texture of 100% whole-grain breads? Try substituting unbleached wheat flour for ½ to ¾ cup of the whole-wheat flour in these breads. Since unbleached flour is refined, your loaf will turn out lighter. Gradually increase the amount of whole-grain flour you use over time. Unbleached flour holds less water than whole wheat flour; so, you'll need to add 1 or 2 extra tablespoons of flour when making substitutions.

Honey-Dijon Rye

	1-pound	1½-pound
whole wheat flour	1⅓ cups	2 cups
rye flour	⅔ cup	1 cup
wheat gluten	4 tsp	2 tbsp
yeast	1 tsp	1½ tsp
sea salt	½ tsp	¾ tsp
lecithin granules or vegetable oil	1 tbsp	1½ tbsp
honey	2 tbsp	3 tbsp
grainy Dijon mustard	2½ tbsp	3 tbsp + 2 tsp
water	⅔ cup	1 cup

Put everything in the machine's bread pan and turn the machine on. A 1-pound loaf makes 12 (1.5 ounce) slices, and a 1½-pound loaf makes 18 slices.

PER SERVING

Calories: 83	Sodium: 123 mg	Cholesterol: 0 mg
Fat: 0.6 g	Protein: 3.1 g	Fiber: 2.6 g

Molasses Rye Bread

	1-pound	1½-pound
whole wheat flour	1¼ cups	1¾ cups + 2 tbsp
rye flour	¾ cup	1 cup + 2 tbsp
wheat gluten	2 tbsp	3 tbsp
yeast	1 tsp	1½ tsp
sea salt	½ tsp	¾ tsp
caraway seeds (optional)	1 tsp	1½ tsp
lecithin granules or vegetable oil	1 tbsp	1½ tbsp
unsulfured molasses	2 tbsp	3 tbsp
water	¾ cup	1 cup + 2 tbsp

Put everything in the machine's bread pan and turn the machine on. A 1-pound loaf makes 12 (1.45 ounce) slices, and a 1½-pound loaf makes 18 slices.

PER SERVING ——————————————————————————

Calories: 85	Sodium: 98 mg	Cholesterol: 0 mg
Fat: 0.9 g	Protein: 3 g	Fiber: 2.6 g

Wheat Germ & Honey Bread

	1-pound	**1½-pound**
whole wheat flour	2 cups	3 cups
toasted wheat germ	3 tbsp	4½ tbsp
wheat gluten	4 tsp	1½ tbsp
yeast	1 tsp	1½ tsp
sea salt	½ tsp	¾ tsp
honey	2 tbsp	3 tbsp
lecithin granules or vegetable oil	1 tbsp	1½ tbsp
water	¾ cup + 1 tbsp	1¼ cup

Put everything in the machine's bread pan and turn the machine on. A 1-pound loaf makes 12 (1.6 ounce) slices, and a 1½-pound loaf makes 18 slices.

PER SERVING ——————————————————————————

Calories: 93	Sodium: 102 mg	Cholesterol: 0 mg
Fat: 1g	Protein: 3.7 g	Fiber: 2.8 g

A Reminder

Variations in humidity or small measurement errors can result in a dough that's either too sticky or too dry. For best results, always check to make sure your dough is properly hydrated. Look at the dough after several minutes of kneading—it should form a soft, smooth, pliable ball. If the dough is too sticky, add more flour, 1 tablespoon at a time. If it's too dry, add more liquid, ½ tablespoon at a time.

Sunflower Granary Bread

	1-pound	1½-pound
whole wheat flour	1⅔ cups	2½ cups
oat bran	¼ cup	¼ cup + 2 tbsp
yellow cornmeal	2 tbsp	3 tbsp
wheat gluten	1½ tbsp	2¼ tbsp
yeast	1 tsp	1½ tsp
sea salt	½ tsp	¾ tsp
unsulfured molasses	2 tbsp	3 tbsp
lecithin granules or vegetable oil	1 tbsp	1½ tbsp
water	¾ cup + 1 tbsp	1¼ cup
sunflower seeds	2 tbsp	3 tbsp

Put everything except sunflower seeds in the machine's bread pan. Turn the machine on to the RAISIN BREAD setting; add the sunflower seeds when the machine buzzes. A 1-pound loaf makes 12 (1.5 ounce) slices, and a 1½-pound loaf makes 18 slices.

PER SERVING

Calories: 90	Sodium: 90 mg	Cholesterol: 0 mg
Fat: 1.8 g	Protein: 3.5 g	Fiber: 2.7 g

Rice Bran Bread

	1-pound	1½-pound
whole wheat flour	1¾ cups	2⅔ cups
rice bran	⅓ cup	½ cup
wheat gluten	1½ tbsp	2¼ tbsp
yeast	¾ tsp	1⅛ tsp
sea salt	½ tsp	¾ tsp
brown-rice syrup or honey	2 tbsp	3 tbsp
lecithin granules or vegetable oil	1 tbsp	1½ tbsp
water	¾ cup	1 cup + 2 tbsp

Put everything in the machine's bread pan and turn the machine on. A 1-pound loaf makes 12 (1.5 ounce) slices, and a 1½-pound loaf makes 18 slices.

This bread is soft-textured and super moist.

PER SERVING

Calories: 86	Sodium: 90 mg	Cholesterol: 0 mg
Fat: 1.4 g	Protein: 3.2 g	Fiber: 2.8 g

Kamut Bread

This ancient strain of wheat, *Kamut,* has all the nutrition of regular whole wheat with a delicate, buttery flavor. Kamut flour may be substituted for regular whole-wheat flour in any recipe.

	1-pound	1½-pound
Kamut flour	2 cups	3 cups
wheat gluten	1 tbsp	1½ tbsp
yeast	1 tsp	1½ tsp
sea salt	½ tsp	¾ tsp
honey	2 tbsp	3 tbsp
lecithin granules or vegetable oil	1 tbsp	1½ tbsp
water	¾ cup + 2 tbsp	1¼ cups + 1 tbsp

Put everything in the machine's bread pan and turn the machine on. A 1-pound loaf makes 12 (1.5 ounce) slices, and a 1½-pound loaf makes 18 slices.

PER SERVING

Calories: 90	Sodium: 90 mg	Cholesterol: 0 mg
Fat: 1 g	Protein: 3.8 g	Fiber: 2.4 g

Variation

Apricot-Pecan Bread Set the machine to the RAISIN BREAD mode. Add ½ cup of chopped dried apricots and ⅓ cup of chopped pecans when the machine beeps. Use ¾ cup of apricots and ½ cup of pecans for a 1½-pound loaf.

Whole Wheat Sour Dough Bread

This recipe is very easy, but you'll have to begin the starter 2 to 3 days in advance.

	1-pound	1½-pound
Starter		
unbleached white flour	½ cup	¾ cup
water	½ cup	¾ cup
sugar	1½ tsp	2¼ tsp
Bread		
whole wheat flour	2 cups	3 cups
wheat gluten	1 tbsp	1½ tbsp
sugar	1 tbsp	1½ tbsp
yeast	¾ tsp	1⅛ tsp
sea salt	½ tsp	¾ tsp
water	½ cup	¾ cup

Two to three days before baking the bread, combine all starter ingredients in a 1-pint glass jar. Stir to mix well; cover loosely with a paper towel, and put the jar in a warm draft-free place (about 80° F). Let the starter sit for 2 to 3 days; stir from time to time, until fermented, bubbly, and sour-smelling. The longer the starter ferments the stronger-tasting your bread will be.

When ready to bake, combine all the bread ingredients in the machine's bread pan. Add all the starter and turn the machine on. A 1-pound loaf makes 12 (1.7 ounce) slices, and a 1½-pound loaf makes 18 slices.

PER SERVING

Calories: 94	Sodium: 90 mg	Cholesterol: 0 mg
Fat: 0.5 g	Protein: 3.5 g	Fiber: 2.7 g

Sourdough Variations

Crusty Round Loaf   Use the RISE setting to let the machine mix and to allow the dough to rise once. Remove the dough from the pan and shape it into a 5-inch round loaf (make a 7-inch round loaf for the 1½-pound recipe). Place it on a baking sheet dusted with cornmeal, and let the dough rise again until it is doubled in bulk. Brush the top with egg white glaze or skim milk, and cut an "X" ¼-inch deep into the top of the loaf. Place a shallow pan half-full of hot water on the lower oven rack. Bake at 400° F for about 25 minutes (30 minutes for a 1½ pound loaf), until golden brown and the bottom sounds hollow when tapped.

Crusty Long Loaf Use the RISE setting to let the machine mix and allow the dough to rise once. Remove the dough from the pan and shape into an 8 × 3-inch oblong loaf (make a 10 × 3-inch loaf for the 1½-pound recipe). Place the loaf on a baking sheet dusted with cornmeal, and let it rise until doubled in bulk. Brush the top with beaten egg white and cut a ¼-inch deep slash lengthwise along the top of the loaf. Place a shallow pan half-full of hot water on the lower oven rack. Bake at 400° F for about 25 minutes for a 1-pound loaf and 30 minutes for a 1½-pound loaf, until golden brown and the bottom sounds hollow when tapped.

Sourdough Rye Substitute rye flour for one-third of the whole wheat flour. Add 1 to 1½ tsp caraway seeds, if desired.

Bran & Oat Bread

	1-pound	1½-pound
whole wheat flour	1⅔ cups	2½ cups
wheat bran	¼ cup	¼ cup + 2 tbsp
quick-cooking rolled oats	¼ cup	¼ cup + 2 tbsp
wheat gluten	1½ tbsp	2¼ tbsp
yeast	1 tsp	1½ tsp
sea salt	½ tsp	¾ tsp
lecithin granules or vegetable oil	1 tbsp	1½ tbsp
white grape juice	1 cup	1½ cups

Put everything in the machine's bread pan and turn the machine on. A 1-pound loaf makes 12 (1.5 ounce) slices, and a 1½-pound loaf makes 18 slices.

PER SERVING

Calories: 87	Sodium: 90 mg	Cholesterol: 0 mg
Fat: 1 g	Protein: 3.3 g	Fiber: 2.7 g

Swedish Rye Bread

	1-pound	1½-pound
whole wheat flour	1⅓ cups	2 cups
rye flour	⅔ cup	1 cup
wheat gluten	2 tbsp	3 tbsp
light brown sugar	1 tbsp	1½ tbsp
yeast	1 tsp	1½ tsp
sea salt	½ tsp	¾ tsp
caraway seeds	¾ tsp	1⅛ tsp
lecithin granules or vegetable oil	1 tbsp	1½ tbsp
orange juice	¾ cup + 2 tbsp	1¼ cups + 1 tbsp

Put everything in the machine's bread pan and turn on the machine. A 1-pound loaf makes 12 (1.6 ounce) slices, and a 1½-pound loaf makes 18 slices.

PER SERVING

Calories: 83	Sodium: 90 mg	Cholesterol: 0 mg
Fat: 0.9 g	Protein: 3.1 g	Fiber: 2.5 g

Corn & Rye Bread

	1-pound	1½-pound
whole-grain cornmeal	¼ cup	¼ cup + 2 tbsp
rye flour	½ cup	¾ cup
whole wheat flour	1¼ cups	1¾ cups + 2 tbsp
wheat gluten	2 tbsp	3 tbsp
yeast	1 tsp	1½ tsp
sea salt	½ tsp	¾ tsp
lecithin granules or vegetable oil	1 tbsp	1½ tbsp
white grape or apple juice	¾ cup + 2 tbsp	1¼ cups + 1 tbsp

Put everything in the machine's bread pan and turn the machine on. A 1-pound loaf makes 12 (1.5-ounce) slices, and a 1½-pound loaf makes 18 slices.

PER SERVING

Calories: 85	Sodium: 90 mg	Cholesterol: 0 mg
Fat: 1 g	Protein: 2.8 g	Fiber: 2.6 g

Russian Black Bread

	1-pound	1½-pound
rye flour	1 cup	1½ cups
whole wheat flour	1 cup	1½ cups
wheat gluten	2 tbsp	3 tbsp
cocoa or carob powder	1½ tbsp	2¼ tbsp
yeast	1 tsp	1½ tsp
sea salt	½ tsp	¾ tsp
unsulfured molasses	2 tbsp	3 tbsp
lecithin granules or vegetable oil	1 tbsp	1½ tbsp
water	¾ cup + 2 tbsp	1¼ cups + 1 tbsp
raisins	½ cup	¾ cup
caraway seeds	½ tsp	¾ tsp

Put everything except the raisins and caraway seeds in the machine's bread pan, and turn the machine to the RAISIN BREAD setting. Add the raisins and caraway seeds when machine buzzes. A 1-pound loaf makes 12 (1.6 ounce) slices, and a 1½-pound loaf makes 18 slices.

PER SERVING

Calories: 109	Sodium: 99 mg	Cholesterol: 0 mg
Fat: 1 g	Protein: 3.2 g	Fiber: 3.3 g

Mexican Cheddar Bread

	1-pound	1½-pound
whole wheat flour	2 cups	3 cups
sugar	2 tsp	1 tbsp
wheat gluten	1 tbsp	1½ tbsp
yeast	1 tsp	1½ tsp
sea salt	½ tsp	¾ tsp
lecithin granules or vegetable oil	1 tbsp	1½ tbsp
whole cumin seed	¾ tsp	1⅛ tsp
nonfat buttermilk	1 cup	1½ cups
shredded nonfat or reduced-fat cheddar cheese	¾ cup	1 cup + 2 tbsp

Put everything except the cheese in the machine's bread pan. Turn the machine on the RAISIN BREAD setting, and add the cheese when the machine buzzes. A 1-pound loaf makes 12 (1.7 ounce) slices, and a 1½-pound loaf makes 18 slices.

PER SERVING ——————————————————————

Calories: 96	Sodium: 161 mg	Cholesterol: 2 mg
Fat: 1.1 g	Protein: 6 g	Fiber: 2.5 g

Vita Bread

	1-pound	1½-pound
water	⅔ cup	1 cup
cabbage	1" wedge	1½" wedge
carrot	4" piece	6" piece
whole wheat flour	2 cups	3 cups
wheat gluten	4 tsp	1½ tbsp
yeast	1 tsp	1½ tsp
sea salt	½ tsp	¾ tsp
lecithin granules or vegetable oil	1 tbsp	1½ tbsp

Put the water, cabbage, and carrot in a blender and process for 1 minute or until vegetables are completely pulverized. Then put this mixture and the remaining ingredients in the machine's bread pan and turn the machine on. A 1-pound loaf makes 12 (1.4 ounce) slices, and a 1½-pound loaf makes 18 slices.

Soft and moist, this bread is also super-nutritious. Sugars naturally present in the carrots and cabbage feed the yeast, eliminating the need for added sugar.

PER SERVING

Calories: 79	Sodium: 92 mg	Cholesterol: 0 mg
Fat: 0.9 g	Protein: 3.2 g	Fiber: 2.7 g

Veggie Bread

	1-pound	1½-pound
whole wheat flour	2 cups	3 cups
wheat gluten	1 tbsp	1½ tbsp
yeast	1 tsp	1½ tsp
sea salt	½ tsp	¾ tsp
lecithin granules or vegetable oil	1 tbsp	1½ tbsp
barley malt or honey	1 tbsp	1½ tbsp
nonfat buttermilk	¾ cup	1 cup + 2 tbsp
grated carrot	¼ cup	¼ cup + 2 tbsp
finely chopped celery	¼ cup	¼ cup + 2 tbsp
finely chopped green onions	2 tbsp	3 tbsp
fresh minced parsley	1 tbsp	1½ tbsp

Put everything in the machine's bread pan and turn the machine on. A 1-pound loaf makes 12 (1.6 ounce) slices, and a 1½-pound loaf makes 18 slices.

PER SERVING

Calories: 87	Sodium: 111 mg	Cholesterol: 0 mg
Fat: 1 g	Protein:3.6 g	Fiber: 2.7 g

Yogurt Oat-Bran Bread

	1-pound	1½-pound
whole wheat flour	1⅔ cups	2½ cups
oat bran	⅓ cup	½ cup
wheat gluten	1½ tbsp	2¼ tbsp
yeast	1 tsp	1½ tsp
sea salt	½ tsp	¾ tsp
nonfat yogurt	½ cup	¾ cup
honey	1 tbsp	1½ tbsp
lecithin granules or vegetable oil	1 tbsp	1½ tbsp
water	⅓ cup	½ cup

Put everything in the machine's bread pan and turn the machine on. A 1-pound loaf makes 12 (1.4 ounce) slices, and a 1½-pound loaf makes 18 slices.

PER SERVING

Calories: 82	Sodium: 97 mg	Cholesterol: 0 mg
Fat: 1 g	Protein: 3.7 g	Fiber: 2.6 g

Amaranth Crunch Bread

	1-pound	1½-pound
whole wheat flour	1⅔ cups	2½ cups
amaranth flour	⅓ cup	½ cup
rolled oats	¼ cup	¼ cup + 2 tbsp
wheat gluten	2 tbsp	3 tbsp
yeast	1 tsp	1½ tsp
sea salt	½ tsp	¾ tsp
lecithin granules or vegetable oil	1 tbsp	1½ tbsp
maple syrup or honey	2 tbsp	3 tbsp
water	¾ cup	1 cup + 2 tbsp
pumpkin seeds	3 tbsp	4½ tbsp

Put everything except the seeds in the machine's bread pan and turn the machine to the RAISIN BREAD setting. Add the seeds when the machine buzzes. A 1-pound loaf makes 12 (1.6 ounce) slices, and a 1½-pound loaf makes 18 slices.

PER SERVING

Calories: 106	Sodium: 91 mg	Cholesterol: 0 mg
Fat: 2.1 g	Protein: 3.9 g	Fiber: 2.4 g

Chick-pea–Sesame Seed Bread

This recipe produces a hearty loaf with a pleasant, nutty flavor.

	1-pound	1½-pound
spelt flour	1⅔ cups	2½ cups
toasted garbanzo (chick-pea) flour	⅓ cup	½ cup
wheat gluten	1 tbsp	1½ tbsp
yeast	1 tsp	1½ tsp
sea salt	½ tsp	¾ tsp
lecithin granules or vegetable oil	1 tbsp	1½ tbsp
plain nonfat yogurt	⅓ cup	½ cup
white grape juice	½ cup	¾ cup
sesame seeds	2 tbsp	3 tbsp

Put everything except the sesame seeds in the machine's bread pan, and turn the machine on the RAISIN BREAD setting. Add the sesame seeds when the machine buzzes. A 1-pound loaf makes 12 (1.4 ounce) slices, and a 1½-pound loaf makes 18 slices.

PER SERVING

Calories: 97	Sodium: 95 mg	Cholesterol: 0 mg
Fat: 2 g	Protein: 4 g	Fiber: 2.2 g

Simply Spelt Bread

Spelt, an ancient grain, makes an exceptional bread flour. Spelt bread rises well without the addition of gluten and has a soft and fine-grain texture. Substitute spelt flour for whole wheat flour in any recipe in this book. Replace each cup of whole wheat flour with 1 cup plus 1 tablespoon of spelt flour.

	1-pound	1½-pound
spelt flour	2 cups	3 cups
yeast	1 tsp	1½ tsp
sea salt	½ tsp	¾ tsp
lecithin granules or vegetable oil	1 tbsp	1½ tbsp
apple juice	¾ cup	1 cup + 2 tbsp

Put everything in the machine's bread pan and turn the machine on. A 1-pound loaf makes 12 (1.5 ounce) slices, and a 1½-pound loaf makes 18 slices.

PER SERVING ————————————————————————————

| Calories: 84 | Sodium: 89 mg | Cholesterol: 0 mg |
| Fat: 1 g | Protein: 2.7 g | Fiber: 1.8 g |

Healthful Additions

For extra flavor and texture, add a few tablespoons of sunflower, pumpkin, sesame, or flax seeds to breads. Chopped walnuts also make a nice addition to breads. Always use the RAISIN BREAD or MIX BREAD setting when adding nuts and seeds to avoid pulverizing them.

What about the fat in nuts and seeds? Unlike margarine, shortening, and other processed fats, nuts and seeds contain fat the way nature intended—packaged with vitamins, minerals, and fiber. Nuts and seeds are rich sources of the antioxidant vitamin E, which protects against cancer, heart disease, and aging.

Wild Rice–Pecan Bread

	1-pound	1½-pound
whole wheat flour	1⅔ cups	2½ cups
brown rice flour	⅓ cup	½ cup
wheat gluten	2 tbsp	3 tbsp
yeast	1 tsp	1½ tsp
sea salt	½ tsp	¾ tsp
lecithin granules or vegetable oil	1 tbsp	1½ tbsp
apple juice	¾ cup + 2 tbsp	1¼ cups + 1 tbsp
cooked wild rice	⅓ cup	½ cup
chopped pecans	¼ cup	¼ cup + 2 tbsp

Put everything except the wild rice and pecans in the machine's bread pan, and turn the machine on the RAISIN BREAD setting. Add the wild rice and pecans when the machine buzzes. A 1-pound loaf makes 12 (1.6 ounce) slices, and a 1½-pound loaf makes 18 slices.

This bread has a nutty taste and great texture.

PER SERVING

Calories: 105   Sodium: 91 mg   Cholesterol: 0 mg
Fat: 2.6 g   Protein: 3.3 g   Fiber: 2.5 g

Applesauce-Raisin Rye

	1-pound	1½-pound
whole wheat flour	1½ cups	2¼ cups
rye flour	½ cup	¾ cup
wheat gluten	1½ tbsp	2¼ tbsp
yeast	1 tsp	1½ tsp
sea salt	½ tsp	¾ tsp
lecithin granules or vegetable oil	1 tbsp	1½ tbsp
unsweetened applesauce	1 cup	1½ cups
raisins	½ cup	¾ cup

Put everything except raisins in the machine's bread pan and turn the machine on the RAISIN BREAD setting. Add the raisins when the machine beeps. A 1-pound loaf makes 12 (1.7 ounce) slices, and a 1½-pound loaf makes 18 slices.

PER SERVING

Calories: 104	Sodium: 91 mg	Cholesterol: 0 mg
Fat: 0.9 g	Protein: 3.2 g	Fiber: 3.2 g

Fruit & Nut Bread

	1-pound	1½pound
whole wheat flour	2 cups	3 cups
wheat gluten	4 tsp	2 tbsp
yeast	1 tsp	1½ tsp
sea salt	½ tsp	¾ tsp
nutmeg	pinch	pinch
lecithin granules or vegetable oil	1 tbsp	1½ tbsp
water	½ cup	¾ cup
mashed banana	½ cup	¾ cup
raisins	⅓ cup	½ cup
chopped walnuts	¼ cup	¼ cup + 2 tbsp

Combine everything except the raisins and walnuts in the machine's bread pan, and turn the machine on the RAISIN BREAD setting. Add the raisins and walnuts when machine buzzes. A 1-pound loaf makes 12 (1.6-ounce slices), and a 1½-pound loaf makes 18 slices.

PER SERVING

Calories: 114	Sodium: 90 mg	Cholesterol: 0 mg
Fat: 2.4 g	Protein: 4 g	Fiber: 3.1 g

Carrot Bread

This carrot bread is slightly sweet and very moist. It's delicious for sandwiches or it can be toasted for a snack anytime.

	1-pound	1½-pound
whole wheat flour	2 cups	3 cups
wheat gluten	4 tsp	2 tbsp
yeast	1 tsp	1½ tsp
sea salt	½ tsp	¾ tsp
lecithin granules or vegetable oil	1 tbsp	1½ tbsp
finely grated carrots	½ cup	¾ cup
toasted wheat germ	3 tbsp	4½ tbsp
apple juice	¾ cup + 2 tbsp	1¼ cups + 1 tbsp

Put everything in the machine's bread pan and turn the machine on. A 1-pound loaf makes 12 (1.6 ounce) slices, and a 1½-pound loaf makes 18 slices.

PER SERVING

Calories: 90	Sodium: 92 mg	Cholesterol: 0 mg
Fat: 1 g	Protein: 3.6 g	Fiber: 2.9 g

Variations

Carrot-Walnut Bread   Use the RAISIN BREAD setting, and add ⅓ cup of chopped walnuts when the machine beeps (use ½ cup of nuts for a 1½-pound loaf).

Carrot-Raisin Bread   Use the RAISIN BREAD setting, and add ½ cup of raisins when the machine beeps (use ¾ cup of raisins for a 1½-pound loaf). For variety, add chopped dates or currants instead of raisins.

Harvest Pumpkin Bread

	1-pound	1½-pound
whole wheat flour	2 cups	3 cups
wheat gluten	4 tsp	2 tbsp
yeast	1 tsp	1½ tsp
sea salt	½ tsp	¾ tsp
maple syrup	2½ tbsp	3 tbsp + 2 tsp
lecithin granules or vegetable oil	1 tbsp	1½ tbsp
cooked mashed pumpkin	⅓ cup	½ cup
water	½ cup + 1 tbsp	⅔ cup + 3 tbsp
pumpkin seeds	3 tbsp	4½ tbsp

Put everything except the pumpkin seeds in the machine's bread pan, and turn the machine on to the RAISIN BREAD setting. Add the seeds when the machine buzzes. A 1-pound loaf makes 12 (1.6 ounce) slices, and a 1½-pound loaf makes 18 slices.

This bread has a super-moist, velvety texture. It makes a delicious sandwich bread.

PER SERVING ——————————————————

| Calories: 107 | Sodium: 92 mg | Cholesterol: 0 mg |
| Fat: 2.4 g | Protein: 4.4 g | Fiber: 2.8 g |

Peanut Butter–Molasses Bread

	1-pound	1½-pound
whole wheat flour	2 cups	3 cups
wheat gluten	1 tbsp	1½ tbsp
yeast	¾ tsp	1⅛ tsp
sea salt	½ tsp	¾ tsp
peanut butter	2 tbsp	3 tbsp
unsulfured molasses	2 tbsp	3 tbsp
water	¾ cup	1 cup + 2 tbsp

Put everything in the machine's bread pan and turn the machine on. A 1-pound loaf makes 12 (1.5 ounce) slices, and a 1½-pound loaf makes 18 slices.

This bread is perfect for peanut butter and banana sandwiches. The protein in peanut butter enhances browning; so, use a light CRUST COLOR setting for this loaf.

PER SERVING

Calories: 92	Sodium: 101 mg	Cholesterol: 0 mg
Fat: 1.8 g	Protein: 3.7 g	Fiber: 2.7 g

Whole Wheat–Banana Nut Bread

This compact, sweet loaf has a cake-like texture; slice thinly. It's delicious toasted and spread with honey.

	1-pound	1½-pound
whole wheat flour	2 cups	3 cups
brown sugar	¼ cup	¼ cup + 2 tbsp
wheat gluten	2 tbsp	3 tbsp
yeast	1 tsp	1½ tsp
sea salt	½ tsp	¾ tsp
lecithin granules or vegetable oil	1 tbsp	1½ tbsp
very ripe mashed banana	1 cup	1½ cups
chopped pecans	⅓ cup	½ cup

Put everything except the pecans in the machine's bread pan. Turn machine on the RAISIN BREAD setting; add the pecans when the machine buzzes. Slice thinly. A 1-pound loaf makes 16 (1.3 ounce) slices, and a 1½-pound loaf makes 24 slices.

PER SERVING

Calories: 97	Sodium: 76 mg	Cholesterol: 0 mg
Fat: 2.3 g	Protein: 2.8 g	Fiber: 2.3 g

Sweet Potato–Apple–Raisin Bread

	1-pound	1½-pound
whole wheat flour	2 cups	3 cups
mashed sweet potato	⅓ cup	½ cup
wheat gluten	1½ tbsp	2¼ tbsp
yeast	1 tsp	1½ tsp
sea salt	½ tsp	¾ tsp
cinnamon	½ tsp	¾ tsp
lecithin granules or vegetable oil	1 tbsp	1½ tbsp
apple juice	⅔ cup	1 cup
golden raisins	½ cup	¾ cup

Put everything except the raisins in the machine's bread pan, and turn the machine on the RAISIN BREAD setting. Add the raisins when machine buzzes. A 1-pound loaf makes 12 (1.8 ounce) slices, and a 1½-pound loaf makes 18 slices.

PER SERVING ————————————————————————

Calories: 111　　Sodium: 96 mg　　Cholesterol: 0 mg

Fat: 0.9 g　　Protein: 3.6 g　　Fiber: 3.1 g

Spiced Apple Bread

	1-pound	1½-pound
whole wheat flour	2 cups	3 cups
wheat gluten	4 tsp	2 tbsp
yeast	1 tsp	1½ tsp
sea salt	½ tsp	¾ tsp
lecithin granules or vegetable oil	1 tbsp	1½ tbsp
apple butter	¾ cup	1 cup + 2 tbsp
water	¼ cup	¼ cup + 2 tbsp

Combine everything in the machine's bread pan and turn the machine on. A 1-pound loaf makes 12 (1.5-ounce slices), and a 1½-pound loaf makes 18 slices. This bread has a sweet and dense cake-like texture. It's delicious toasted and spread with nonfat ricotta or cream cheese. Use the SWEET bread setting if your machine has one.

PER SERVING

Calories: 88	Sodium: 101 mg	Cholesterol: 0 mg
Fat: 1.3 g	Protein: 3.7 g	Fiber: 2.7 g

Apricot-Raisin-Almond Bread

	1-pound	**1½-pound**
whole wheat flour	2 cups	3 cups
wheat gluten	1 tbsp	1½ tbsp
yeast	1 tsp	1½ tsp
sea salt	½ tsp	¾ tsp
cinnamon	⅓ tsp	½ tsp
lecithin granules or vegetable oil	1 tbsp	1½ tbsp
apricot nectar	¾ cup + 2 tbsp	1¼ cups + 1 tbsp
chopped, dried apricots	¼ cup	¼ cup + 2 tbsp
raisins	¼ cup	¼ cup + 2 tbsp
chopped almonds	¼ cup	¼ cup + 2 tbsp

Combine everything except the apricots, raisins, and almonds in the machine's bread pan. Turn the machine on the RAISIN BREAD setting. Add the apricots, raisins, and almonds when the machine buzzes. A 1-pound loaf makes 16 (1.7-ounce slices), and a 1½-pound loaf makes 18 slices.

PER SERVING

Calories: 114	Sodium: 91 mg	Cholesterol: 0 mg
Fat: 2.3g	Protein: 3.8 g	Fiber: 3.4 g

Oatmeal Raisin Bread

	1-pound	1½-pound
whole wheat flour	1½ cups	2¼ cups
oat flour	½ cup	¾ cup
wheat gluten	1½ tbsp	2¼ tbsp
yeast	1 tsp	1½ tsp
sea salt	½ tsp	¾ tsp
lecithin granules or vegetable oil	1 tbsp	1½ tbsp
honey or unsulfured molasses	2 tbsp	3 tbsp
water	¾ cup	1 cup + 2 tbsp
raisins	½ cup	¾ cup

Put everything except the raisins in the machine's bread pan, and turn the machine on the RAISIN BREAD setting. Add the raisins when the machine buzzes. A 1-pound loaf makes 12 (1.6 ounce) slices, and a 1½-pound loaf makes 18 slices.

PER SERVING

Calories: 98   Sodium: 91 mg   Cholesterol: 0 mg

Fat: 0.6 g   Protein: 3.4 g   Fiber: 2.7 g

Shapely Loaves

THE RISE, DOUGH, or MANUAL feature on your breadmaker programs the machine to mix, knead, and raise the dough once. When the dough is ready to be shaped, the machine will beep to let you know. This allows you to make an infinite variety of beautifully shaped breads.

Tips & Tricks

Shape dough on a lightly floured surface. If it seems a little sticky, knead in a bit of flour. After shaping, cover loosely with a dishtowel and put the dough in a warm place (85 to 90° F) for the second rising.

How do you know when the loaf has completed its second rising and is ready for baking? Gently press into the dough with your fingertip. The dough should feel spongy and your finger indentation should slowly fill in. If the space fills in quickly, it's not ready. If the space does not fill in, you've waited too long. It's better to bake bread dough a little short of its second rising than to wait too long.

Finishing Touches

For a crusty, shiny glaze, brush tops lightly and evenly with **egg white glaze** (1 egg white beaten with 1 tablespoon of water) just before baking. Or make this **eggless glaze**: Combine ½ cup of water, 1 teaspoon of cornstarch, and 1 teaspoon of honey. Bring the mixture to a boil in a small pot. Cook and stir for a few minutes, until clear. You'll only need about 1 tablespoon per loaf; refrigerate leftovers up to a week.

If you prefer a soft, golden finish, brush loaves with a little skim milk (instead of egg white) just before baking. Soy milk works as well as dairy cow's milk.

For a lovely finish, sprinkle rolled oats, oat bran, or wheat bran over the tops of loaves before baking. Poppy seeds, sesame seeds, wheat germ, finely chopped nuts, and minced onion also make nice toppings.

How Do You Know It's Done?

If you are not used to baking bread, knowing when it is done can indeed be confusing. Here are some good indicators:

- Fully cooked bread shrinks slightly from the sides of the pan. It should also slide out of the pan easily.

- Squeeze the sides—they should feel springy and resilient. Your squeeze shouldn't leave indentations in the loaf.

- Tap the bottom—if the bread is done, it should sound hollow, not muffled.

- Insert a thermometer into the loaf's center. Fully cooked bread will register 190° F.

- The top should be nicely browned. Beware, though, that browning is not always a good indicator of doneness because the top can become brown before the center is fully cooked. If you find the loaf is browned to your satisfaction but not completely done, place a piece of foil loosely over the top of the loaf during the remaining baking time. This will prevent overbrowning.

Italian Flatbread

This hearty bread is similar to thick and chewy pizza crust. It's good with soup, pasta, or salad.

	1- or 1½-pound
whole wheat flour	1 cup
bread flour	1 cup
yeast	1½ tsp
sea salt	½ tsp
sugar	2 tsp
skim milk or water	¾ cup
olive oil	1½ tsp
Dijon mustard	1½ tsp
crushed garlic	2 tsp
dried crushed oregano	1 tsp
onion, quartered and thinly sliced	1 medium

Put the first six ingredients in the machine's bread pan. Turn the machine on the RISE setting, so that the machine will mix, knead, and allow the dough to rise once. Remove the dough and shape it into two balls. Roll each into a 7-inch circle on a floured surface. Place the dough on a baking sheet coated with cooking spray.

Combine the olive oil, mustard, and garlic; spread it over the dough. Sprinkle with oregano and sliced onions. If you wish, sprinkle a little grated parmesan over top. Bake at 400° F for about 15 minutes or until golden brown. Cut the bread into wedges to serve. This recipe makes 16 pieces.

PER SERVING

Calories: 62	Sodium: 79 mg	Cholesterol: 0 mg
Fat: 0.3 g	Protein: 2.3 g	Fiber: 1.2 g

Whole Wheat Egg Bread

	1- or 1½-pound
whole wheat flour	2½ cups
wheat gluten	1½ tbsp
honey	2 tbsp
yeast	1½ tsp
sea salt	½ tsp
egg substitute*	¼ cup + 2 tbsp
lecithin granules or vegetable oil	1 tbsp
nonfat buttermilk	¾ cup + 2 tbsp

*Use 2 large, whole eggs instead of egg substitute, if you wish.

Put everything in machine's bread pan. Turn the machine on the RISE setting, so that the machine mixes, kneads, and allows the dough to rise once. Turn the dough onto a lightly floured surface, and shape it into three 12-inch ropes. Braid the ropes together and pinch the ends to seal them. Place the braid on a baking sheet coated with cooking spray.

Cover with a towel and let the bread rise in a warm place until it is doubled in size—about 45 minutes. Brush top of loaf with some egg white glaze and sprinkle with poppy seeds if desired. Bake at 350 degrees for about 30 minutes, until golden brown. Makes 16 slices.

PER SERVING

Calories: 85	Sodium: 89 mg	Cholesterol: 0 mg
Fat: 0.8 g	Protein: 3.8 g	Fiber: 2.4 g

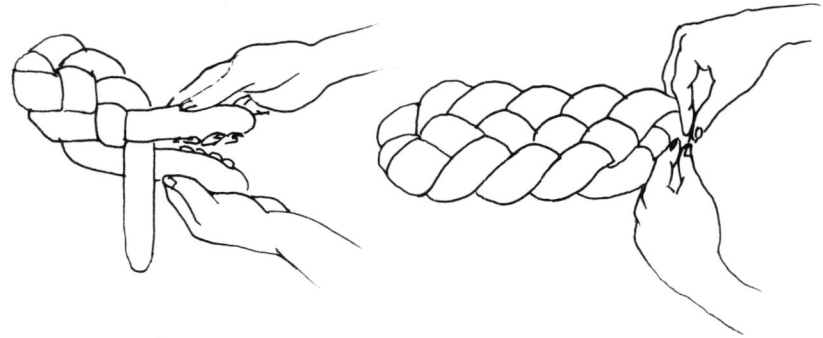

Pesto Bread

	1- or 1½-pound
whole wheat flour	1 cup
bread flour	1 cup
yeast	1 tsp
sugar	1 tsp
sea salt	½ tsp
water	¾ cup
moderately packed, fresh basil leaves	⅓ cup
fresh, minced parsley	3 tbsp
grated parmesan	¼ cup
pine nuts or chopped walnuts	2 tbsp
crushed garlic	1 tsp
lemon juice	2 tsp

Place the first six ingredients in the machine's bread pan. Turn the machine on the RISE setting so that it will mix, knead, and allow the dough to rise once. Turn the dough onto a lightly floured surface, and roll it into a 10 × 12-inch rectangle.

Put the remaining ingredients in a food processor, and process them into a paste. Spread half of this mixture along the center third of the dough (along the 12-inch length). Fold the bottom third of the dough over the filling. Top this layer with the remaining pesto. Fold the top third of the dough over the filling.

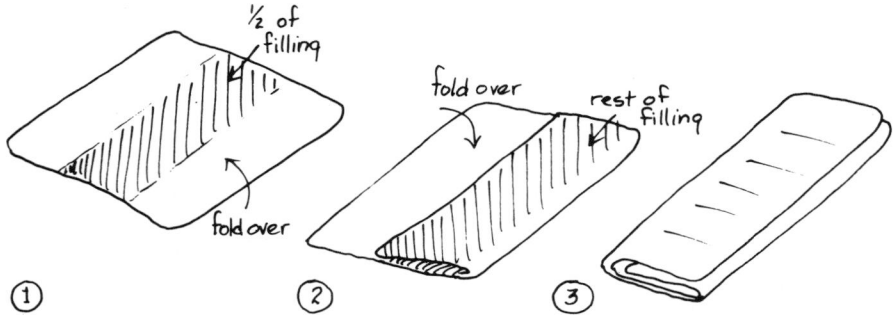

Place the loaf on a baking sheet coated with cooking spray. Use a sharp knife to cut into the dough at 1-inch intervals. Cut through to the bottom layer of dough, but do not cut all the way through. Brush the top with egg white glaze or skim milk, if desired. Bake at 400° F for 12 to 15 minutes or until the top is light golden brown. This recipe makes 12 pieces.

PER SERVING

Calories: 91	Sodium: 129	Cholesterol: 2 mg
Fat: 1.5 g	Protein: 3.7 g	Fiber: 1.7 g

Kamut French Bread

The delicate, buttery flavor of Kamut is perfect for French bread.

	1- or 1½-pound
Kamut flour	1¼ cups
bread flour	1 cup
sugar	1 tbsp
yeast	¾ tsp
sea salt	½ tsp
water or skim milk	¾ cup + 2 tbsp
egg white glaze	1 tbsp

Put everything except the egg white in the machine's bread pan. Turn the machine on the RISE setting, so that it will mix, knead, and allow the dough to rise. When the dough has risen, shape it into a 16-inch cylindrical loaf or two 8-inch loaves. Place the dough on a baking sheet dusted with cornmeal.

Cover it with a towel, and let it rise at *room temperature* about 1¼ hours, until doubled in bulk. A cooler, longer rise develops French bread flavor best. Brush the top with the egg white glaze. Use a serrated knife to cut diagonal slashes every 3 inches across the top. Put a shallow pan of hot water on the bottom oven rack. Bake at 400° F for 15 to 20 minutes, until golden brown. This recipe makes 12 (1½-inch) slices.

PER SERVING

Calories: 81	Sodium: 90 mg	Cholesterol: 0 mg
Fat: 0.4 g	Protein: 3 g	Fiber: 2 g

Hearty Grain Bread

	1- or 1½-pound
rolled wheat, rye, or oat flakes	½ cup
wheat bran	¼ cup
water	1 cup + 3 tbsp
whole wheat flour	2 cups
wheat gluten	2 tbsp
yeast	1½ tsp
sea salt	½ tsp
unsulfured molasses	3 tbsp
lecithin granules or vegetable oil	1 tbsp
sunflower seeds or chopped walnuts	¼ cup
flax seeds or sesame seeds	2 tbsp

Combine the first three ingredients in a small pot. Bring them to a boil; cook and stir for 30 seconds. Allow the mixture to cool to room temperature. Put the flour and the next five ingredients in the machine's bread pan; add the cooked mixture. Turn the machine on the RISE setting. Let the machine work the dough for a few minutes; then, add another tablespoon of water, if needed. Add the sunflower seeds and flax seeds after about 12 minutes, or when the machine signals.

When the dough has risen, shape it into a 7 × 10-inch oval. With the side of your hand, crease down its length, just off center. Fold the smaller side over the larger side. Place the dough on a large baking sheet coated with cooking spray. Cover and allow it to rise in a warm place until doubled in size (about 45 minutes). Brush the top with egg white glaze or skim milk and sprinkle with wheat bran if desired. Bake at 350° F for 25 to 30 minutes, until the top is golden brown and the bottom sounds hollow when tapped. This recipe makes 16 (1.5-ounce) slices.

PER SERVING

Calories: 91	Sodium: 66 mg	Cholesterol: 0 mg
Fat: 2.2 g	Protein: 2.8 g	Fiber: 2.8 g

Swiss Onion-Herb Bread

	1- or 1½-pound
whole wheat flour	1½ cups
rye flour	½ cup
wheat gluten	1½ tbsp
yeast	1½ tsp
sea salt	½ tsp
honey or barley malt	1 tbsp
lecithin granules or vegetable oil	1 tbsp
water	¾ cup + 1 tbsp
shredded, reduced-fat Swiss cheese	1 cup
fresh, minced onion	2 tbsp
dried, crushed thyme	¾ tsp
dried, crushed marjoram	¾ tsp

Put the first eight ingredients in the machine's bread pan. Turn the machine on the RISE setting so that it will mix, knead, and allow the dough to rise once. Add the remaining ingredients after about 12 minutes, or when the machine signals.

After the dough has risen, turn it onto a lightly floured surface, and shape it into an 8 × 3-inch oblong loaf. Place the dough on a baking sheet coated with cooking spray. Cover the dough and allow it to rise in a warm place until doubled in size—about 45 minutes. Brush the top with egg white glaze or skim milk and slash the loaf diagonally at 2-inch intervals. Bake at 350° F for 25 to 30 minutes, until the top is lightly browned and the bottom sounds hollow when tapped. This recipe makes 12 (1.8-ounce) slices.

PER SERVING

Calories: 113	Sodium: 168 mg	Cholesterol: 10 mg
Fat: 2.5 g	Protein: 5.9 g	Fiber: 2.5 g

Black Rye Bread

	1- or 1½-pound
whole wheat flour	1 cup
rye flour	1 cup
cocoa powder	1 tbsp
wheat gluten	2 tbsp
yeast	1½ tsp
sea salt	½ tsp
caraway seeds	1 tsp
unsulfured molasses	2 tbsp
lecithin granules or vegetable oil	1 tbsp
room-temperature coffee	¾ cup + 1 tbsp

Put everything in the machine's bread pan. Turn the machine on the RISE setting so that it mixes, kneads, and allows the dough to rise once. After the dough has risen, turn it onto a lightly floured surface and shape it into a 7-inch oblong loaf. Place on a baking sheet coated with cooking spray.

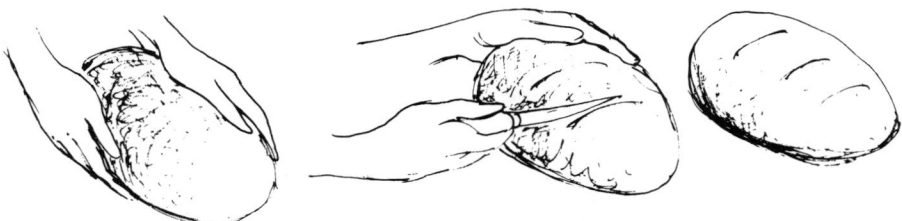

Cover the dough and allow it to rise in a warm place until doubled in size—about 45 minutes. Brush top with egg white glaze or skim milk and slash diagonally at 2-inch intervals. Bake at 350° F for 25 to 30 minutes, until the bottom sounds hollow when tapped. This recipe makes 12 (1.4-ounce) slices.

PER SERVING

Calories: 82	Sodium: 94 mg	Cholesterol: 0 mg
Fat: 0.9 g	Protein: 2.8 g	Fiber:2.7 g

Sprouted Wheat Bread

Chew carefully; wheat sprouts in the crust are crunchy.

	1- or 1½-pound
whole wheat flour	2 cups
wheat gluten	1 tbsp
yeast	¾ tsp
sea salt	½ tsp
barley malt or honey	1 tbsp
lecithin granules or vegetable oil	1 tbsp
water	¾ cup + 1 tbsp
wheat sprouts	½ cup

Put everything except the wheat sprouts in your machine's bread pan. Turn the machine on the RISE setting so that it will mix, knead, and allow the dough to rise once. Add the wheat sprouts after about 12 minutes, or when the machine signals.

After the dough has risen, turn it onto a lightly floured surface and shape it into a round loaf 5 inches in diameter. Place the dough on a baking sheet coated with cooking spray.

Cover and let it rise in a warm place until doubled in size—about 35 minutes. Brush the top with egg white glaze or skim milk, and cut 4 slashes in a tic-tac-toe design across the top. Bake at 350° F for about 25 minutes, until the top is golden brown and the bottom sounds hollow when tapped. This makes 12 (1.5-ounce) slices.

PER SERVING ——————————————————————————————————————

Calories: 90	Sodium: 91 mg	Cholesterol: 0 mg
Fat: 1 g	Protein: 3.4 g	Fiber: 2.9 g

Cottage Dill Bread

	1- or 1½-pound
whole wheat flour	1½ cups
unbleached flour	1 cup
wheat gluten	1½ tbsp
sugar	2 tsp
yeast	1¼ tsp
sea salt	½ tsp
lecithin granules or vegetable oil	1 tbsp
nonfat or low-fat cottage cheese	½ cup
water	½ cup + 1 tbsp
finely chopped onion	2½ tbsp
dried dill seed	1 tbsp

Put everything in the machine's bread pan. Turn the machine on to the RISE setting so that the machine will mix, knead, and allow the dough to rise once. After the dough has risen, turn it onto a lightly floured surface, and shape it into a round loaf 5 inches in diameter. Place the loaf in an 8-inch round pan coated with cooking spray.

Cover and let the dough rise in a warm place until doubled in size—about 35 minutes. Brush the top with egg white glaze or skim milk and cut an "X" slash in the top with a serrated knife. Bake at 350° F for 30 minutes, until the top is golden brown and the bottom sounds hollow when tapped. This recipe makes 16 (1.3-ounce) slices.

PER SERVING

Calories: 80	Sodium: 96 mg	Cholesterol: 0 mg
Fat: 0.5 g	Protein: 3.6 g	Fiber: 1.7 g

Spinach & Cheese Loaf

	1- or 1½-pound
bread flour	1⅔ cups
oat bran	¾ cup
sugar	1 tbsp
yeast	2 tsp
sea salt	½ tsp
water	¾ cup
mustard	2 tbsp
frozen chopped spinach, thawed	10-ounce package
grated parmesan cheese	3 tbsp
shredded reduced-fat Swiss cheese	1¼ cups

Put the first seven ingredients in the machine's bread pan. Turn the machine on the RISE setting so that the machine will mix, knead, and allow the dough to rise once. After the dough has risen, turn it onto a lightly floured surface, and shape the dough into a 9 × 12-inch rectangle. Place the dough on a baking sheet coated with cooking spray.

Spread half of the shredded cheese over the center third of the rectangle along the 12-inch length. Squeeze the excess water from the spinach; combine the spinach and parmesan cheese, and spread it over the shredded Swiss cheese. Top with the remaining shredded Swiss cheese.

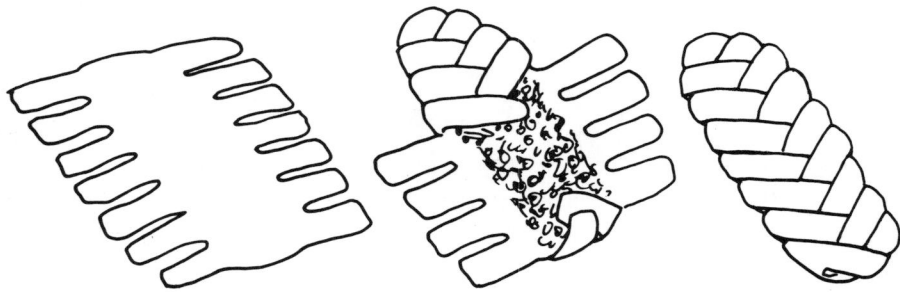

With a sharp knife, make cuts from the filling to the dough edges at 1-inch intervals along sides of filling. Alternating sides, fold strips at an angle over the filling. Cover and allow the dough to rise in a warm, draft-free place until it is doubled in size—about 30 minutes. Brush the top with egg white glaze or skim milk. Bake at 375° F for about 25 minutes, until golden brown. Serve warm. This loaf makes 12 slices.

PER SERVING

Calories: 131	Sodium: 193 mg	Cholesterol: 7 mg
Fat: 3.2 g	Protein: 7.8 g	Fiber: 2.1 g

Sweet Potato Braid

	1- or 1½-pound
whole wheat flour	2 cups
wheat gluten	2 tbsp
brown sugar	2 tbsp
yeast	1½ tsp
sea salt	½ tsp
dried, grated orange rind	1 tsp
lecithin granules or vegetable oil	1 tbsp
mashed sweet potatoes	½ cup
orange juice	⅔ cup

Put everything in the machine's bread pan. Turn the machine on the RISE setting so that it will mix, knead, and allow the dough to rise once. Turn the dough onto a lightly floured surface, and divide it into 3 pieces. Roll each piece into a 22-inch rope. Braid the ropes together and bring the ends around to form a circle. Pinch the ends together to seal.

Place in a 9-inch round pan coated with cooking spray. Cover the dough with a towel, and allow it to rise in a warm place until doubled in size—35 to 45 minutes. Brush the top with skim milk or egg white glaze. Bake at 350° F for about 25 minutes, until the top is golden brown. This recipe makes 12 servings. Serve the braid warm with orange marmalade or nonfat cream cheese.

PER SERVING

Calories: 104	Sodium: 119 mg	Cholesterol: 0 mg
Fat: 0.9 g	Protein: 3.8 g	Fiber: 2.7 g

Orange-Pecan Tea Loaves

This is delicious served warm with nonfat cream cheese.

Dough	**1- or 1½-pound**
whole wheat flour	2¼ cups
oat bran	¼ cup
wheat gluten	1½ tbsp
yeast	1½ tsp
sea salt	½ tsp
dried, grated orange rind	¾ tsp
lecithin granules or vegetable oil	1 tbsp
orange juice	1 cup + 2 tbsp
Filling	
orange marmalade	¼ cup
chopped pecans	⅓ cup

Put the dough ingredients in the machine's bread pan and turn it on the RISE setting. When the dough has risen, divide it into two pieces and roll each into an 8 × 8-inch rectangle on a lightly floured surface. Spread half the marmalade over each piece to within ½ inch of the edges and sprinkle the pecans over top. Roll it up like a jelly roll.

Place each loaf seam side down in a 7½ × 3¾-inch loaf pan coated with cooking spray; tuck the ends under slightly. Cover and allow the dough to rise in a warm place until it's doubled in bulk—about 35 minutes. Bake at 350° F for 20 to 25 minutes, until light golden brown. This recipe makes 18 (¾-inch) slices.

PER SERVING

Calories: 87	Sodium: 60 mg	Cholesterol: 0 mg
Fat: 2.2 g	Protein: 2.8 g	Fiber: 2.3 g

Cinnamon-Swirl Bread

	1- or 1½-pound
whole wheat flour	2½ cups
wheat gluten	4 tsp
yeast	1¼ tsp
sea salt	½ tsp
lecithin granules or vegetable oil	4 tsp
apple juice	1 cup + 3 tbsp
honey	3 tbsp
cinnamon	1½ tsp
raisins or dates (optional)	⅓ cup

Put the first six ingredients in the machine's bread pan. Turn the machine on the RISE setting so that it will mix, knead, and allow the dough to rise once.

When the dough has risen, turn it onto a floured surface, and roll it out into an 8 × 18-inch rectangle. Drizzle with the honey and sprinkle with the cinnamon; use a spoon to spread the honey and cinnamon evenly over dough. Sprinkle with the raisins or dates if desired. Roll up the dough like a jelly roll from the short end. Tuck the ends under and place the seam side down in an 8 × 4-inch loaf pan coated with cooking spray.

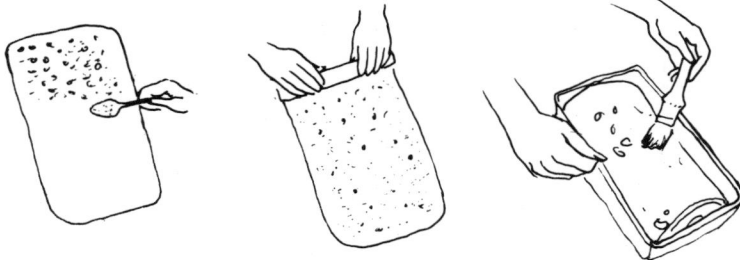

Cover and let the dough rise in a warm place until doubled in bulk—about 1 hour. Brush the top with egg white glaze or skim milk. Bake at 350° F for 25 to 30 minutes, until golden brown. This recipe makes 16 (½-inch) slices.

PER SERVING

Calories: 92	Sodium: 68 mg	Cholesterol: 0 mg
Fat: 1 g	Protein: 2.9 g	Fiber: 2.4 g

Stollen

This traditional holiday bread is delicious all year round.

	1- or 1½-pound
bread flour	1¼ cups
whole wheat flour	½ cup
oat flour	½ cup
yeast	1½ tsp
sea salt	½ tsp
dried, grated lemon rind	¾ tsp
pear or apricot nectar	½ cup + 2 tbsp
egg substitute or whole egg	3 tbsp
margarine or butter	1 tbsp
golden raisins	¼ cup
currants or chopped dates	¼ cup
chopped, dried apricots	¼ cup
chopped almonds	¼ cup

Put all ingredients except the fruits and almonds in the machine's bread pan. Turn the machine on the RISE setting so that the machine will mix, knead, and allow the dough to rise once. Add the fruits and almonds after 12 minutes, or when the machine signals.

After the dough has risen, turn it onto a floured surface. Shape it into a 6½ × 8-inch oval. With the side of your hand, crease the oval down its length, just off center. Fold the smaller side over the larger side. Place the loaf on a baking sheet coated with cooking spray.

Cover the dough with a towel and let it rise in a warm place until doubled in size—about 1 hour. Brush the top lightly with egg white glaze or skim milk. Bake at 350° F for about 30 minutes, until the top is golden brown and the bottom sounds hollow when tapped. This recipe makes 16 (1.4-ounce) slices.

PER SERVING

Calories: 106	Sodium: 82 mg	Cholesterol: 0 mg
Fat: 2.2 g	Protein: 3 g	Fiber: 1.9 g

Maple-Walnut Loaf

The loaf is slightly sweet with a nutty crunch. For variety, substitute buckwheat flour for one-fourth of the whole-wheat flour.

	1- or 1½-pound
whole wheat flour	2 cups
wheat gluten	1½ tbsp
yeast	1½ tsp
sea salt	½ tsp
nutmeg	⅛ tsp
lecithin granules or vegetable oil	1 tbsp
maple syrup	¼ cup
water	½ cup + 2 tbsp
lemon juice	2 tsp
chopped walnuts	⅓ cup

Put everything except the walnuts in the machine's bread pan. Turn the machine on the RISE setting so that it will mix, knead, and allow the dough to rise once. Add the nuts after 12 minutes, or when the machine signals.

After the dough has risen, shape it into a 7-inch oblong loaf. Place the dough on a baking sheet coated with cooking spray. Cover it with a towel and allow it to rise in a warm, draft-free place until doubled in size—about 45 minutes. Brush the top lightly with egg white glaze or skim milk. With a sharp knife, slash the top of the loaf diagonally at 2-inch intervals. Bake at 350° F for 25 to 30 minutes, until the top is golden brown and the bottom sounds hollow when tapped. This loaf makes 12 slices.

PER SERVING

Calories: 111	Sodium: 90 mg	Cholesterol: 0 mg
Fat: 2.3 g	Protein: 4.3 g	Fiber: 2.7 g

Buns, Biscuits & Bagels

THE *RISE, DOUGH,* or *MANUAL* feature on your breadmaker programs the machine to mix, knead, and allow the dough to rise once. When the dough is ready to be shaped, the machine will beep to let you know. This allows you to make an infinite variety of shaped rolls, biscuits, and buns. All of these recipes can be made in either 1-pound or 1½-pound machines.

For Best Results

Most of these recipes require the dough to rise a second time after the dough is shaped. To facilitate the dough rising a second time, cover the shaped dough with a towel and place it in a warm spot (85 to 90° F) for the specified time. If the room is cool, heat your oven slightly; then turn it off. Put the dough in the warm oven with the door closed to rise.

Near the end of the suggested rising period, check the dough to see if it's ready to bake. Gently press into the dough with your fingertip. It should feel spongy, and the indentation left by your finger should fill in slowly. If the space fills in quickly, it isn't ready. If the space does not fill in, you have waited too long.

Some recipes call for **egg white glaze** (1 egg white beaten with 1 tablespoon of water) brushed on top before baking. Also see Finishing Touches on p. 60.

Multibran Buns

	1- or 1½-pound
oat bran	¼ cup
rice bran	¼ cup
wheat bran	¼ cup
bread flour	1¾ cups
whole wheat flour	¼ cup
toasted wheat germ	3 tbsp
yeast	1¼ tsp
sea salt	½ tsp
water	¾ cup + 1 tbsp
honey or unsulfured molasses	2 tbsp

Put everything in the machine's bread pan. Turn the machine on the RISE setting so that it will mix, knead, and allow the dough to rise once. When the dough has risen, turn it onto a lightly floured surface, and shape it into twelve balls. Arrange them 1 inch apart on a baking sheet coated with cooking spray. Cover and let them rise in a warm place until doubled in size—about 35 minutes.

Brush the tops lightly with skim milk or egg white glaze, and sprinkle some wheat bran over the tops. Bake at 350° F for 12 to 15 minutes, until tops are lightly browned. This recipe makes 12 buns.

PER SERVING

Calories: 106	Sodium: 88 mg	Cholesterol: 0 mg
Fat: 0.9 g	Protein: 3.4 g	Fiber: 2.7 g

Cornmeal Crescents

	1- or 1½-pound
whole wheat flour	1 cup
whole-grain cornmeal	¼ cup
bread flour	1¼ cups
yeast	2 tsp
sea salt	½ tsp
honey or unsulfured molasses	2 tbsp
margarine or butter	1 tbsp
skim milk	¾ cup + 2 tbsp

Put everything in the machine's bread pan. Turn the machine on the RISE setting. When the dough has risen, divide it into two pieces, and roll each piece into a 12-inch circle on a lightly floured surface. Cut each circle into eight wedges. Roll each wedge up from the wide end, and place it point side down on a baking sheet coated with cooking spray; bring the ends around slightly to form a crescent.

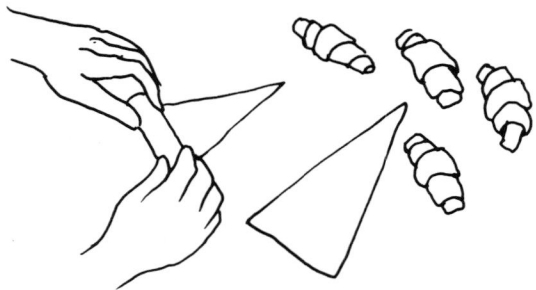

Cover and let the crescents rise in a warm place for about 30 minutes, until doubled in size. Brush the tops with skim milk or beaten egg white if desired. Bake at 375° F for 10 minutes, until the tops are lightly browned. This recipe makes sixteen crescents.

PER SERVING

Calories: 184	Sodium: 85 mg	Cholesterol: 0 mg
Fat: 1 g	Protein: 2.6 g	Fiber: 1.4 g

Variation

Orange-Pecan Crescents Combine ½ cup of finely chopped pecans and ¼ cup of orange marmalade. Put 1½ teaspoons of this mixture in the center of the wide end of each crescent. Roll it up and bake as directed. These crescents are perfect for brunch.

Raisin-Rye Rolls

	1- or 1½-pound
rye flour	1 cup
whole wheat flour	½ cup
bread flour	1 cup + 2 tbsp
yeast	1½ tsp
sea salt	½ tsp
prune or apple juice	1 cup
raisins	½ cup
caraway seeds	1 tsp

Put everything except the raisins and seeds in the machine's bread pan. Turn the machine on the RISE setting. After 12 minutes or when the machine signals, add the raisins and seeds. When dough has risen, turn it onto a lightly floured surface and shape it into 12 balls. Arrange the rolls 1½ inches apart in a baking pan coated with cooking spray.

Cover the rolls and let them rise in a warm place for about 30 minutes, until doubled in size. Brush the tops with skim milk or egg white glaze. Use a sharp knife to make a ½-inch deep "X" in the top of each roll. Bake at 350° F for 15 minutes, until tops are lightly browned. This recipe makes 12 rolls.

PER SERVING

Calories: 98	Sodium: 92 mg	Cholesterol: 0 mg
Fat: 0.5 g	Protein: 3.1 g	Fiber: 1.8 g

Feathery Whole Wheat Biscuits

	1- or 1½-pound
whole wheat pastry flour	1½ cups
unbleached flour	1 cup
yeast	1½ tsp
baking powder	1½ tsp
baking soda	½ tsp
sugar	1 tbsp
nonfat or low-fat cottage cheese	1 cup
water	¼ cup

Put everything in the machine's bread pan. Turn the machine on and let it knead the dough for 4 to 5 minutes, just until ingredients are well mixed. Turn the dough onto a floured surface, and roll it out to ½-inch thickness. Cut biscuits out with a 2½-inch cutter. Place the biscuits on a baking sheet coated with cooking spray. For soft biscuits, arrange with sides barely touching; for crusty biscuits, space 1 inch apart.

Cover and let the dough rise in a warm place until doubled in size, about 30 minutes. Bake at 375° F for 8 to 10 minutes, until the tops are touched with golden brown. Check the bottoms for browning to prevent overbaking. This recipe makes 10 large biscuits.

PER SERVING ——————————————————————

Calories: 126	Sodium: 194 mg	Cholesterol: 0 mg
Fat: 0.5 g	Protein: 6.6 g	Fiber: 2.5 g

Variation

Raisin Breakfast Biscuits   Add ½ cup of raisins to the dough ingredients.

Pull-Apart Poppy Seed Rolls

	1-or 1½-pound
whole wheat flour	1¼ cups
bread flour	1 cup
honey	2 tbsp
yeast	1 tsp
sea salt	½ tsp
skim milk	¾ cup
poppy seeds	1–2 tsp

Put everything except the poppy seeds in the machine's bread pan. Turn the machine on to the RISE setting, so that it will mix, knead, and allow the dough to rise once. Turn the dough onto a lightly floured surface, and shape it into 12 balls. Arrange the balls in a 9-inch round pan coated with cooking spray.

Cover them with a towel and let them rise in a warm place until doubled in size (about 30 minutes). Brush the tops with egg white glaze or skim milk and sprinkle them with the poppy seeds. Bake at 350° F for 15 to 18 minutes, until lightly browned. This recipe makes 12 rolls.

PER SERVING

Calories: 96	Sodium: 102 mg	Cholesterol: 0 mg
Fat: 0.9 g	Protein: 3.9 g	Fiber: 1.6 g

Oatmeal Dinner Rolls

	1 or 1½-pound
oat flour	½ cup
whole wheat flour	¾ cup
bread flour	1¼ cups
yeast	1¼ tsp
sea salt	½ tsp
honey or maple syrup	2 tbsp
nonfat buttermilk	¾ cup + 2 tbsp

Put everything in the machine's bread pan. Turn the machine on the RISE setting. When the dough has risen, turn it onto a lightly floured surface and shape it into 12 balls. Arrange the rolls 1½ inches apart in a baking pan coated with cooking spray. Cover the rolls and let them rise in a warm place for about 35 minutes, until doubled in size.

Brush tops with skim milk or egg white glaze. Use a sharp knife to make a ½-inch deep slash through the top of each roll. Sprinkle rolled oats or oat bran over tops. Bake at 350° F for 12 to 15 minutes, until the tops are lightly browned. This recipe makes 12 rolls.

PER SERVING

Calories: 106	Sodium: 109 mg	Cholesterol: 0 mg
Fat: 1 g	Protein: 4.2 g	Fiber: 1.9 g

Currant-Cardamom Rolls

	1- or 1½-pound
whole wheat flour	1¼ cups
bread flour	1 cup
yeast	1½ tsp
sea salt	½ tsp
ground cardamom	½ tsp
white grape juice	¾ cup + 2 tbsp
lecithin granules or vegetable oil	1 tbsp
currants	½ cup

Put everything except currants in the machine's bread pan. Turn the machine on the RISE setting, so that it will mix, knead, and allow the dough to rise once. Add the currants after 12 minutes or when the machine signals. Remove the dough and turn it onto a lightly floured surface; shape it into 12 balls. Arrange the balls 1½ inches apart in a baking pan coated with cooking spray.

Cover with a towel and let them rise in a warm place until doubled in size, about 30 minutes. Brush the tops with egg white glaze or skim milk. Bake at 350° F for 15 to 18 minutes, until lightly browned. This recipe makes 12 rolls.

PER SERVING

Calories: 111	Sodium: 91 mg	Cholesterol: 0 mg
Fat: 0.9 g	Protein: 3.1 g	Fiber: 2.3 g

Amaranth-Oatmeal Rolls

	1- or 1½-pound
whole wheat flour	¾ cup
amaranth flour	¼ cup
quick-cooking rolled oats	¼ cup
bread flour	1 cup + 2 tbsp
yeast	1½ tsp
sea salt	½ tsp
honey	1½ tbsp
lecithin granules or vegetable oil	1 tbsp
water	¾ cup

Put everything in the machine's bread pan. Turn the machine on the RISE setting, so that it will mix, knead, and allow the dough to rise once. Remove the dough, and turn it onto a lightly floured surface; shape it into 9 balls. Arrange the balls 2 inches apart in a baking pan coated with cooking spray.

Cover them with a towel and let them rise in a warm place until doubled in size, about 30 minutes. Brush the tops with egg white glaze or skim milk. Use a sharp knife to make a ½-inch deep "X" in the top of each roll. Sprinkle the tops with rolled oats. Bake at 350° F for 15 to 18 minutes, until lightly browned. This recipe makes 9 rolls.

PER SERVING

Calories: 128	Sodium: 120 mg	Cholesterol: 0 mg
Fat: 1.3 g	Protein: 3.9 g	Fiber: 2.1 g

Honey Whole Wheat Bagels

	1- or 1½-pound
whole wheat flour	3 cups
wheat gluten	2 tbsp
yeast	2 tsp
sea salt	1 tsp
water	1 cup
honey	3 tbsp

Put everything in the machine's bread pan. Turn the machine on the RISE setting, so that it will mix, knead, and allow the dough to rise once. Turn the dough onto a lightly floured surface and shape it into eight balls. Shape each ball into an 8-inch rope. Bring the ends around to form a ring, overlap the ends by ½ inch, and work the ends together to seal. Let the bagels rest 5 minutes while you put a large pot of water on the stove to boil.

Place four bagels at a time in the boiling water and boil for 1 minute. Remove them with a slotted spoon and place them on a baking sheet coated with cooking spray. If desired, brush the tops of the bagels with egg white glaze and sprinkle them with sesame seeds, poppy seeds, or onion flakes. Bake at 350° F for about 25 minutes, until golden brown. This recipe makes 8 bagels.

PER SERVING

Calories: 179	Sodium: 269 mg	Cholesterol: 0 mg
Fat: 0.9 g	Protein: 6 g	Fiber: 5.7 g

Variations

Oat Bran Bagels Substitute oat bran for ¾ cup of the whole wheat flour.

Raisin Bagels Knead ⅔ cup of raisins into the finished dough.

Russian Raisin-Rye Bagels

	1- or 1½-pound
whole wheat flour	2 cups
rye flour	½ cup
cocoa or carob powder	1½ tbsp
wheat gluten	1½ tbsp
yeast	1½ tsp
sea salt	½ tsp
caraway seeds	½ tsp
water	1 cup + 1 tbsp
unsulfured molasses	2 tbsp
raisins	½ cup

Put everything except the raisins in the machine's bread pan. Turn the machine on the RISE setting, so that it will mix, knead, and allow the dough to rise once. Add the raisins after 12 minutes or when the machine signals. When the dough has risen, turn it onto a lightly floured surface, and shape it into six balls. Shape each ball into an 8-inch rope; bring the ends around to form a ring, overlap the ends by ½ inch, and work the ends together to seal. Let the bagels rest for 5 minutes while you put a large pot of water on to boil.

Place three bagels at a time in the boiling water, and boil them for 1 minute. Remove them with a slotted spoon, and place them on a baking sheet coated with cooking spray. If desired, brush the tops with egg white glaze. Bake at 350° F for 25 minutes, until golden brown. This recipe makes 6 bagels.

PER SERVING

Calories: 234	Sodium: 192 mg	Cholesterol: 0 mg
Fat: 1.2 g	Protein: 8 g	Fiber: 7.5 g

Sprouted Wheat Bagels

Enzymes in the wheat sprouts release natural sugars from the flour, eliminating the need for added sugar.

	1- or 1½-pound
whole wheat flour	2½ cups
wheat gluten	1½ tbsp
yeast	1½ tsp
sea salt	½ tsp
water	1 cup + 1 tbsp
wheat sprouts	⅓ cup

Put everything in the machine's bread pan. Turn the machine on the RISE setting, so that it will mix, knead, and allow the dough to rise once. When the dough has risen, turn it onto a lightly floured surface, and shape it into six balls. Shape each ball into an 8-inch rope. Bring the ends around to form a ring, overlap the ends by ½ inch, and work the ends together to seal. Let the bagels rest 5 minutes while you put a large pot of water on to boil.

Place three bagels at a time in the boiling water, and boil them for 1 minute. Remove them with a slotted spoon, and place them on a baking sheet coated with cooking spray. Brush the tops with egg white glaze, if desired. Bake at 350° F for about 25 minutes, until golden brown. This recipe makes six bagels.

PER SERVING

Calories: 190	Sodium: 181 mg	Cholesterol: 0 mg
Fat: 1 g	Protein: 8.2 g	Fiber: 6.8 g

Whole Wheat English Muffins

	1- or 1½-pound
whole wheat flour	2 cups
honey or barley malt	1 tbsp
yeast	2 tsp
sea salt	¾ tsp
skim milk	1 cup − 1 tbsp
cornmeal	2 to 5 tablespoons

Put everything except the cornmeal in the machine's bread pan. Turn the machine on the RISE setting, so that it will mix, knead, and allow the dough to rise once. The dough should be fairly soft; add a little more flour if necessary. When dough has risen, turn it onto a lightly floured surface and roll out to ½-inch thick. Cut out six muffins with a 3½-inch round cutter (a glass custard cup works well). Coat both sides with cornmeal (moisten tops if necessary to make it stick).

Cover the muffins with a towel and let them rise for 30 minutes, until doubled in bulk. Cook them on an ungreased griddle at 325° F for 20 to 25 minutes, until deep brown on both sides. Turn them every 5 minutes. Cool them on a rack. This recipe makes six muffins.

PER SERVING

Calories: 156	Sodium: 289 mg	Cholesterol: 0 mg
Fat: 0.9 g	Protein: 6.7 g	Fiber: 5 g

Whole Wheat Burger Buns

	1- or 1½-pound
whole wheat flour	2 cups
yeast	1¼ tsp
sea salt	½ tsp
honey	1 tbsp
nonfat buttermilk	¾ cup + 2 tbsp

Put everything in the machine's bread pan. Turn the machine on the RISE setting so that it will mix, knead, and allow the dough to rise once. After the dough has risen, turn it onto a lightly floured surface. Roll out the dough to ½-inch thick, and cut out six buns with a 3½-inch cutter (a glass custard cup works well). Place the buns on a baking sheet coated with cooking spray.

Cover and allow them to rise in a warm place until they're doubled in size—about 30 minutes. Brush the tops with skim milk or egg white glaze, if desired, and sprinkle sesame seeds, poppy seeds, or finely chopped onions over the tops. Bake at 375° F for about 12 minutes, until the tops are lightly browned. This recipe makes six (2.9-ounce) buns.

PER SERVING

Calories: 163	Sodium: 217 mg	Cholesterol: 0 mg
Fat: 1.6 g	Protein: 6.7 g	Fiber: 5 g

Amaranth Energy Bars

These energizing bars make a great breakfast on the run. If you have a 1½- or 2-pound machine, make a double batch and freeze some for later. Microwave the bars to reheat them.

	1- or 1½-pound
whole wheat flour	2 cups
amaranth flour	½ cup
wheat gluten	1 tbsp
yeast	1¼ tsp
sea salt	½ tsp
cinnamon	¼ tsp
unsweetened applesauce	1 cup
raisins	½ cup
chopped walnuts	¼ cup

Put everything except the raisins and walnuts in the machine's bread pan. Turn the machine on the RISE setting. After about 12 minutes or when the machine signals, add the raisins and walnuts.

When the dough has risen, turn it onto a lightly floured surface and shape it into eight balls. Roll each ball into a 5-inch rope. Arrange them 2 inches apart on a baking sheet coated with cooking spray. For chewy, bagel-like bars, bake them immediately at 375° F for about 10 minutes. For soft bars, cover them, and let them rise in a warm place for about 30 minutes, until doubled in size. Bake at 375° F for about 10 minutes, until the tops are lightly browned. This recipe makes 8 bars.

PER SERVING

Calories: 202	Sodium: 137 mg	Cholesterol: 0 mg
Fat: 3.3 g	Protein: 7 g	Fiber: 5.3 g

Brown-Rice–Banana Buns

Sweetened naturally with bananas and dates, these buns are great with breakfast or for a snack anytime.

	1- or 1½-pound
whole wheat flour	2 cups
brown rice flour	½ cup
wheat gluten	1½ tbsp
sea salt	½ tsp
yeast	1½ tsp
mashed banana	¾ cup
lecithin granules or vegetable oil	1 tbsp
water	½ cup
chopped dates	½ cup
chopped walnuts (optional)	¼ cup

Put everything except the dates and walnuts in the machine's bread pan. Turn the machine on the RISE setting. After about 12 minutes or when the machine signals, add the dates and walnuts. When the dough has risen, turn it onto a lightly floured surface and shape it into 12 balls. Arrange the balls in a baking pan coated with cooking spray. For soft rolls, arrange the balls with sides barely touching, for crusty rolls, arrange them 1 inch apart.

Cover and let them rise in a warm place for about 30 minutes, until doubled in size. Bake at 350° F for 20 minutes, until the tops are golden brown. This recipe makes 12 buns.

PER SERVING ————————————

Calories: 127	Sodium: 90 mg	Cholesterol: 0 mg
Fat: 1.1 g	Protein: 3.9 g	Fiber: 3.5 g

Sesame Pita Bread

	1- or 1½-pound
whole wheat flour	2 cups
wheat gluten	1 tbsp
honey	1 tsp
yeast	1 tsp
sea salt	½ tsp
water	¾ cup
sesame tahini	1 tbsp

Combine everything in the machine's bread pan. Turn the machine on the RISE setting so that it will mix, knead, and allow the dough to rise once. Make sure the dough is properly hydrated; it should form a smooth ball. Adjust the liquid or flour as needed.

When the dough has risen, shape it into eight balls. Then roll each ball into a 5-inch circle; cover them and let them rise for 30 minutes. Place the bread directly on the racks in a 475° F oven.

Bake for 2 to 4 minutes, until puffed up. Cool them on racks. This recipe makes eight pitas. For a fat-free pita bread, add another ½ tablespoon of water instead of the sesame tahini.

PER SERVING ————————————

Calories: 119	Sodium: 136 mg	Cholesterol: 0 mg
Fat: 1.5 g	Protein: 5 g	Fiber: 4 g

Barley-Herb Breadsticks

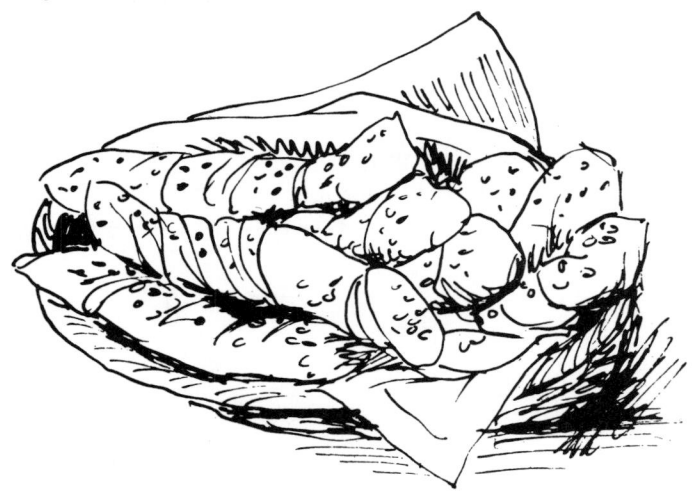

Dough	**1- or 1½-pound**
bread flour	1¼ cups
whole wheat flour	¾ cup
barley flour	½ cup
sugar	1 tbsp
yeast	2 tsp
sea salt	½ tsp
water	¾ cup
egg white	1
Topping	
olive oil	1 tbsp
crushed garlic	½ tsp
dried rosemary	1 tsp

Put everything in the machine's bread pan. Turn the machine on the RISE setting so that it will mix, knead, and allow the dough to rise once. After the dough has risen, turn it onto a lightly floured surface. Divide the dough into twelve pieces and shape each piece into a 12-inch rope. Fold each rope in half, twist it several times, and pinch the ends to seal.

Place the breadsticks on a baking sheet coated with cooking spray. For chewy breadsticks, let the breadsticks sit for 15 minutes. For soft breadsticks, cover them and let them rise until doubled in bulk. Combine the topping ingredients and brush the mixture over tops. Bake at 400° F for 8 to 10 minutes. This recipe makes 12 breadsticks.

PER SERVING

Calories: 105   Sodium: 94 mg   Cholesterol: 0 mg

Fat: 1.5 g   Protein: 3.1 g   Fiber: 2.1 g

Versatile Refrigerator Doughs

C ONVENIENT AND VERSATILE, refrigerator doughs enable you to have
fresh, hot bread anytime. These doughs can be stored in the refrigerator
for up to 2 days. Refrigerator doughs are perfect when you are cooking
for just one or two, because you can pinch off just the amount you need to make
a variety of hot and delicious breads. Use a food scale to weigh the appropriate
amount of dough.

Oat-Bran Refrigerator Dough

	1-pound	1½-pound
bread flour	2 cups	3 cups
oat bran	1 cup	1½ cups
yeast	2 tsp	1 tbsp
sea salt	¾ tsp	1⅛ tsp
sugar	1 tbsp	1½ tbsp
lecithin granules or vegetable oil	4 tsp	2 tbsp
skim milk or water	1 cup + 1 tbsp	1½ cups + 2 tbsp

Put everything in the machine's bread pan, and turn the bread machine on its RISE setting. Remove the dough after 25 minutes. Place the dough in a large bowl coated with cooking spray. Cover and refrigerate the dough for at least 6 hours and up to 2 days. You may also freeze the dough and thaw it when you're ready to use it. When ready to use, proceed with any of these variations; use a food scale to weigh the required amount of dough. The smaller machine makes 1¼ pounds of dough; the larger machine makes about 1¾ pounds.

Cheese Broccoli Stuffs

Roll a 3-ounce ball of **Oat-Bran Refrigerator Dough** into a 6-inch circle. Spread **3 tablespoons of chopped, fresh or frozen (thawed) broccoli** along the middle. Top with **2 tablespoons of shredded nonfat or reduced-fat mozzarella, Swiss, Provolone, or cheddar cheese.** Fold both edges toward the center, overlapping slightly to enclose the filling. Arrange them 2 inches apart on baking sheets coated with cooking spray. Bake them immediately at 450° F for about 8 minutes, until lightly browned.

PER SERVING

Calories: 210	Sodium: 344 mg	Cholesterol: 3 mg
Fat: 2.5 g	Protein: 12 g	Fiber: 3.6 g

Poppy Seed Pretzels

Pinch off 2-ounce pieces of **Oat-Bran Refrigerator Dough** for each pretzel. Roll each piece into a 14-inch rope and twist it into a pretzel shape. Place the pretzels on a baking sheet coated with cooking spray. Cover and let them rise until they're doubled in bulk, about 45 minutes. For chewy pretzels, bake immediately—do not allow them to rise. Brush each pretzel lightly with **egg white glaze**, and sprinkle them with ¼ tsp of **poppy seeds**. Bake at 375° F for 8 to 10 minutes.

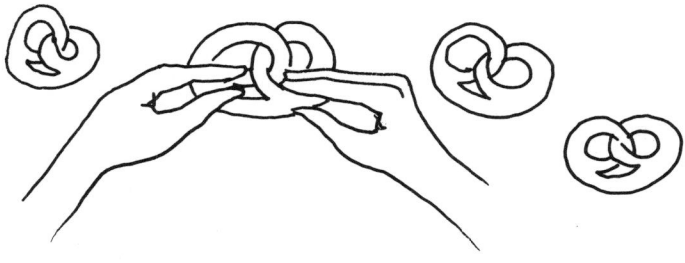

PER SERVING

Calories: 123	Sodium: 160 mg	Cholesterol: 0 mg
Fat: 1.5 g	Protein: 4.6 g	Fiber: 2.1 g

Parmesan Twists

Pinch off 2-ounce pieces of **Oat-Bran Refrigerator Dough** for each twist. Shape each piece into a 15-inch rope. Fold the rope in half and twist it together. Place the twists on a baking sheet coated with cooking spray. Cover them and let them rise until they're doubled in bulk, about 45 minutes. Brush each twist lightly with **skim milk** and sprinkle them with **1 teaspoon of grated Parmesan cheese**. Bake at 375° F for 8 to 10 minutes.

PER SERVING

Calories: 133	Sodium: 198 mg	Cholesterol: 2 mg
Fat: 2 g	Protein: 5.5 g	Fiber: 2.1 g

Personal Pan Pizza

Roll a 4-ounce ball of **Oat-Bran Refrigerator Dough** into a 6½-inch circle. Place the circle in the bottom of a 6-inch cast-iron skillet lightly coated with **olive oil**. Top the pizza with these ingredients in the order listed—**2 tablespoons of tomato sauce, ⅓ cup of shredded nonfat or reduced-fat mozzarella cheese, 1 tablespoon of chopped green pepper, 1 thin slice of onion separated into rings,** and **½ teaspoon of dried, crushed oregano.** Bake at 475° F for 8 to 10 minutes, until the cheese is bubbly and lightly browned. This recipe makes 1 serving.

PER SERVING

Calories: 316	Sodium: 591 mg	Cholesterol: 7 mg
Fat: 3.3 g	Protein: 22 g	Fiber: 5.2 g

Spinach & Cheese Calzones

Combine a **10-ounce package of frozen, chopped spinach** (thawed and squeezed dry), **1 cup of nonfat ricotta cheese,** and **½ teaspoon of dried, crushed Italian seasoning.** Set aside. Pinch off 12 ounces of **Oat-Bran Refrigerator Dough.** Divide the dough into four pieces, and turn it onto a floured surface. Shape each piece into a ball and roll it into a 7 to 8-inch circle.

Place one-fourth of the spinach mixture on the lower half of each circle, and sprinkle with **2 tablespoons of shredded nonfat or reduced-fat mozzarella cheese.** Moisten the edges of the dough with water; bring the top half over the bottom half and pinch edges to seal. Place the calzones on a baking sheet coated with cooking spray, and bake them at 400° F for 18 to 20 minutes, until golden brown. Serve with a side dish of **marinara sauce,** if desired. This recipe makes four calzones.

PER SERVING

Calories: 271	Sodium: 459 mg	Cholesterol: 3 mg
Fat: 2.6 g	Protein: 2.2 g	Fiber: 4.7 g

Hot Apple Turnovers

Combine **1 cup of finely chopped apple, ¼ cup of apple juice, ¼ cup of raisins, 1 tablespoon of sugar,** and **¼ teaspoon of cinnamon** in a small pot. Cover the pot and allow the mixture to simmer for 5 minutes. Stir **1 tablespoon of cornstarch** into **1 tablespoon of apple juice**, and add it to the apple mixture. Cook and stir for 1 minute until thickened. Cool to room temperature.

Pinch off 10 ounces of **Oat-Bran Refrigerator Dough.** Divide the dough into 5 pieces, and roll each piece into a 5-inch circle. Put 2½ tablespoons of filling on the bottom half of each circle. Fold the top half over the bottom half to enclose the filling. Crimp the edges with a fork to seal. Arrange the turnovers 2 inches apart on a baking sheet coated with cooking spray. Brush the tops with **skim milk**, and sprinkle them with some **cinnamon sugar**. Bake immediately at 375° F for 18 to 20 minutes, until lightly browned. Serve warm.

PER SERVING

Calories: 187	Sodium: 162 mg	Cholesterol: 0 mg
Fat: 1.7 g	Protein: 5 g	Fiber: 3.3 g

Oat-Bran Crescents

Pinch off 12 ounces of **Oat-Bran Refrigerator Dough** and roll it into a 12-inch circle on a lightly floured surface. Cut the dough into eight wedges. Roll each wedge up from the wide end and place it point side down on a baking sheet coated with cooking spray. Cover the crescents and let them rise until doubled in bulk, about 45 minutes. Brush each crescent lightly with **egg white glaze**. Bake them at 350° F for 10 to 12 minutes, until lightly browned.

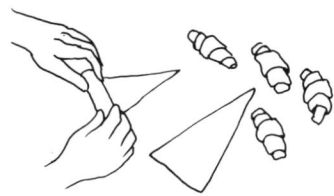

PER SERVING

Calories: 98	Sodium: 120 mg	Cholesterol: 0 mg
Fat: 1.2 g	Protein: 3.5 g	Fiber: 1.6 g

Jam & Cheese Foldovers

Roll out 2-ounce balls of **Oat-Bran Refrigerator Dough** into 5-inch circles. Spread **2 teaspoons of nonfat** or **reduced-fat cream cheese** along the center of each circle to within 1 inch of each end. Top with **1 teaspoon of your favorite jam or preserves**. Fold both edges toward the center, overlapping slightly to enclose the filling. Arrange the foldovers 2 inches apart on baking sheets coated with cooking spray. Cover and let them rise until doubled in bulk, about 45 minutes. Bake at 375° F for 10 minutes or until lightly browned. Serve warm. A serving is 1 foldover.

PER SERVING

Calories: 152	Sodium: 227 mg	Cholesterol: 2 mg
Fat: 1.6 g	Protein: 6.7 g	Fiber: 2.2 g

Berry Delicious Coffee Cake

Combine ¼ **cup of sugar** and **2 tablespoon of cornstarch** in a saucepan. Stir in ¼ **cup of apple juice** and 1½ **cups of fresh or frozen blueberries, raspberries, or blackberries**. Cook and stir over medium heat for several minutes, until thickened and bubbly. Set aside to cool.

Roll a pound of **Oat-Bran Refrigerator Dough** into a 12 × 9-inch rectangle on a lightly floured surface. Transfer the dough to a baking sheet coated with cooking spray. Spoon the filling down the center third of the dough. On each side of the filling, cut twelve 1-inch strips from the edge of the filling to the outer edge of the dough. Alternating sides, fold strips at an angle across the filling to suggest a braided look.

Cover and let the dough rise in a warm place until doubled in bulk—35 to 45 minutes. Brush the top with **egg white glaze**. Sprinkle **2 to 3 teaspoons of sugar** over top. Bake at 350° F for 20 to 25 minutes, until lightly browned. Serve warm. This recipe makes 12 servings.

PER SERVING

Calories: 105	Sodium: 106 mg	Cholesterol: 0 mg
Fat: 1 g	Protein: 3.1 g	Fiber: 1.5 g

Jammin' Breakfast Buns

Pinch off 9 ounces of **Oat-Bran Refrigerator Dough** and shape into six balls. Arrange the balls in an 8-inch round baking pan. Cover the buns and let them rise in a warm place until doubled in bulk, about 35 minutes. Make a depression in the center of each bun, and fill it with **1½ teaspoons of fruit preserves**. Bake at 350° F for 12 to 14 minutes. This recipe makes 6 buns.

PER SERVING ——————————————————————

Calories: 109	Sodium: 107 mg	Cholesterol: 0 mg
Fat: 1 g	Protein: 3.1 g	Fiber: 1.5 g

Potato Refrigerator Dough

	1-pound	1½-pound
whole wheat flour	2⅓ cups	3½ cups
instant mashed potato flakes	⅔ cup	1 cup
wheat gluten	1 tbsp	1½ tbsp
sugar	2 tbsp	3 tbsp
yeast	1½ tsp	2 tsp
sea salt	¾ tsp	1 tsp
lecithin granules or vegetable oil	4 tsp	2 tbsp
water	1 cup	1½ cups

Put everything in the machine's bread pan, and turn the machine on the RISE setting. Remove the dough after 25 minutes. Place the dough in a large bowl coated with cooking spray. Cover the dough and refrigerate for at least 6 hours and up to two days. You may also freeze the dough and thaw it when you're ready to use it. When ready to use, proceed with any of these variations; use a food scale to weigh the required amount of dough. The smaller bread machine makes 1⅓ pounds of dough; the larger machine makes 2 pounds.

Apricot Coffee Buns

Combine ⅔ **cup of chopped dried apricots** and ⅔ **cup of orange juice** in a pot. Cover and simmer for 10 minutes, until the liquid is absorbed. Set the mixture aside to cool. Pinch off 12 ounces of **Potato Refrigerator Dough**; turn the dough onto a floured surface, and roll it into a 9 × 12-inch rectangle. Spread the dough with apricot filling, then roll it up like a jelly roll from the long end.

Place the seam side down on a baking sheet coated with cooking spray, and shape it into a semicircle. Use scissors to snip into the dough at every 1-inch interval. Twist the slices so that the cut sides are up. Cover and let rise until doubled in bulk, about one hour. Bake at 350° F for 18 to 20 minutes, until golden brown.

Make a glaze of ¼ **cup of powdered sugar**, ½ **teaspoon of almond extract**, and 1½ **teaspoons of skim milk**. Spoon glaze over the warm buns. Serve warm. This recipe makes 12 buns.

PER SERVING

Calories: 91	Sodium: 79 mg	Cholesterol: 0 mg
Fat: 0.7 g	Protein: 2.5 g	Fiber: 2.3 g

Cinnamon-Raisin Rolls

Pinch off 12 ounces of **Potato Refrigerator Dough**. Turn the dough onto a floured surface and roll it into an 8 × 8-inch square. Brush 1½ **tablespoons of honey** over the dough. Sprinkle with **1 teaspoon of cinnamon** and **3 tablespoons of raisins**. Roll the dough up like a jelly roll.

Cut the dough into eight pieces, and place them on a pan coated with cooking spray. Cover the rolls and let them rise until they're doubled in bulk, about 45 minutes. Bake at 350° F for 16 to 18 minutes, until light golden brown. Combine ¼ **cup of powdered sugar**, ¼ **teaspoon of vanilla**, and 1½ **teaspoons of skim milk**; drizzle over the warm rolls. Serve warm. This recipe makes 8 rolls.

PER SERVING

Calories: 125	Sodium: 119 mg	Cholesterol: 0 mg
Fat: 0.9 g	Protein: 3.3 g	Fiber: 2.8 g

Date & Cheese Coffee Cake

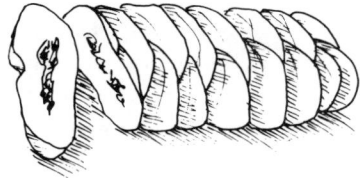

Roll out a pound of **Potato Refrigerator Dough** into a 12 × 9-inch rectangle on a lightly floured surface. Transfer the dough to a baking sheet coated with cooking spray. Stir together **6 ounces of softened nonfat** or **reduced-fat cream cheese, 2 tablespoons of sugar, ½ teaspoon of vanilla, and ½ cup of chopped dates.** Spoon the filling down the center third of the dough.

On each side of the filling, cut twelve 1-inch strips from the edge of the filling to the outer edge of the dough. Alternating sides, fold strips at an angle across the filling to give the coffee cake a braided look.

Brush the top with **skim milk** and sprinkle it with a little **sugar.** Cover the coffee cake and let it rise until doubled in bulk—about 45 minutes. Bake at 350° F for 20 to 25 minutes, until lightly browned. Serve warm. This recipe makes 12 servings.

PER SERVING

Calories: 115	Sodium: 205 mg	Cholesterol: 2 mg
Fat: 0.9 g	Protein: 6 g	Fiber: 3 g

Bow-Knot Dinner Rolls

Pinch off 2-ounce pieces of **Potato Refrigerator Dough** for each roll. Shape each piece into a 9-inch rope and loosely tie it into a knot. Place the rolls on a baking sheet coated with cooking spray. Cover them with a towel and let them rise until doubled in bulk, about 45 minutes. Bake at 350° F for about 15 minutes, until lightly browned.

PER SERVING

Calories: 119	Sodium: 158 mg	Cholesterol: 0 mg
Fat: 1.1 g	Protein: 4 g	Fiber: 3.5 g

Pull-Apart Sesame Seed Rolls

Pinch off twelve (1½-ounce) pieces of **Potato Refrigerator Dough** and shape each into a ball. Arrange the balls in a 9-inch round pan coated with cooking spray. Cover them with a towel and let them rise in a warm place until doubled in size, about 45 minutes. Brush the tops with **egg white glaze** and sprinkle them with **sesame seeds**. Bake at 350° F for 16 to 18 minutes, until lightly browned. This recipe makes 12 rolls.

PER SERVING

Calories: 92	Sodium: 118 mg	Cholesterol: 0 mg
Fat: 1.1 g	Protein: 3.3 g	Fiber: 2.7 g

Pizza Perfection

WHOLE GRAIN CRUSTS, nonfat and reduced-fat cheeses, and lots of vegetable toppings make these pizzas perfect for a healthful and hearty meal anytime. Making pizza for just one or two people? Use only the amount of dough you need for a smaller pizza. Refrigerate the remaining dough for up to 3 days to make more pizza later on.

All of these recipes can be made in either 1-pound or 1½-pound machines. However, if you have a 1½-pound machine, you have the option of making a slightly larger pizza, if you wish. To do this, multiply the ingredients by 1.5.

Veggie-Patch Pizza

Crust	**1- or 1½-pound**
whole wheat or oat flour	1 cup
bread flour	1 cup
sugar	1 tsp
sea salt	½ tsp
yeast	1¼ tsp
celery seed	½ tsp
water	¾ cup
Toppings	
tomato paste	¼ cup
crushed garlic	1 tsp
plum tomato, thinly sliced	1 medium
shredded nonfat or reduced-fat mozzarella cheese	1 cup
fresh broccoli florets	¼ cup
sliced yellow squash	¼ cup
sliced mushrooms	¼ cup
thin slices of onion, separated into rings	2–3
dried, crushed Italian seasoning	1 tsp
grated Parmesan cheese	2 tbsp

Put the crust ingredients in the machine's bread pan. Use the RISE setting, so that the machine will mix, knead, and allow the dough to rise. Lightly oil a 12-inch cast-iron skillet with olive oil. Turn the dough onto a floured surface and roll it out into a circle slightly bigger than the bottom of the skillet. Place the dough in the skillet. Combine the tomato paste and garlic and spread over the crust. Add toppings in the order listed. Bake at 475° F 13 to 15 minutes. This recipe makes 8 slices.

PER SERVING ————————————————————————————

Calories: 150	Sodium: 300 mg	Cholesterol: 4 mg
Fat: 1.2 g	Protein: 9.4 g	Fiber: 3.2 g

Fiesta Pizza

Crust	1- or 1½-pound
whole wheat flour	¾ cup
bread flour	1 cup
whole-grain cornmeal	¼ cup
water	¾ cup
yeast	1½ tsp
sea salt	½ tsp
sugar	1 tsp
Toppings	
tomato sauce	⅓ cup
chili powder	½ tbsp
shredded nonfat or reduced-fat Monterey Jack cheese	¾ cup
shredded nonfat or reduced-fat mozzarella cheese	½ cup
thin slices of onion, separated into rings	3
chopped jalapeño pepper	2 tbsp
sliced black olives	2 tbsp

Put the crust ingredients in the machine's bread pan. Use the RISE setting so that the machine will mix, knead, and allow the dough to rise. When the dough has risen, turn it onto a floured surface, and roll it into a 12-inch circle. Place the dough on a 12-inch pizza pan dusted with cornmeal. Mix the tomato paste and chili powder and spread it over the dough. Top the crust with the remaining topping ingredients in the order listed. Bake at 475° F for about 10 minutes, until the cheese is lightly browned and bubbly. This recipe makes 8 slices.

PER SERVING

Calories: 144	Sodium: 350 mg	Cholesterol: 3 mg
Fat: 0.8 g	Protein: 9 g	Fiber: 2.8 g

Florentine Stuffed Pizza

Crust	**1- or 1½-pound**
whole wheat flour	1½ cups
bread flour	1½ cups
yeast	2 tsp
sea salt	¾ tsp
water	1 cup
olive oil	1 tbsp
Filling	
tomato paste	⅓ cup
crushed garlic	1 tsp
frozen, chopped spinach (thaw and squeeze dry)	5 ounces
shredded nonfat or reduced-fat mozzarella cheese	1 cup
artichoke hearts, quartered	1 cup
red-bell-pepper strips	⅓ cup
grated Parmesan cheese	2 tbsp
dried, crushed Italian seasoning	1 tsp

Put the crust ingredients in the machine's bread pan. Use the RISE setting so that the machine will mix, knead, and allow the dough to rise. Roll the dough into a 15-inch circle. Place it on a 14-inch pizza pan coated with cooking spray, and form a rim of dough around the edges.

Cut a 7-inch "X" in the center of the dough. Cut another "X" to form eight wedges in the center. Combine the tomato paste and garlic, and spread the mixture in a 3-inch-wide border evenly around the edges of dough. Top the tomato paste with the remaining ingredients in the order listed. Pull the cut points of dough over the filling. Moisten the points with water and tuck under the outer rim. Press firmly to seal. Bake at 425° F for 15 to 18 minutes. This recipe makes 8 slices.

PER SERVING

Calories: 229	Sodium: 391 mg	Cholesterol: 4 mg
Fat: 5.4 g	Protein: 12 g	Fiber: 5.8 g

Spinach Pesto Pizzas

Crust	1- or 1½-pound
whole wheat or oat flour	1 cup
bread flour	1 cup
sugar	1 tsp
sea salt	½ tsp
yeast	1½ tsp
water	¾ cup
Toppings	
fresh spinach (packed)	½ cup
fresh basil (packed)	⅓ cup
grated Parmesan cheese	¼ cup
crushed garlic	1 tsp
lemon juice	2 tsp
olive oil	1 tsp
plum tomatoes, thinly sliced	2–3
shredded, reduced-fat mozzarella cheese	1½ cups

Put the crust ingredients in the machine's bread pan. Use the RISE setting, so that the machine will mix, knead, and allow the dough to rise. To make the pesto, put the spinach and the next five ingredients in a food processor and process them into a paste; set aside.

When the dough has risen, turn it onto a floured surface and divide it into six pieces. Roll each piece into a 5-inch circle. Arrange a thin layer of tomatoes over each crust and spread it with 2½ teaspoons of pesto. Top each with ¼ cup of mozzarella. Place the pizzas on a baking sheet coated with cooking spray. Bake at 450° F for 8 to 10 minutes. This recipe makes 6 pizzas.

PER SERVING

Calories: 221	Sodium: 470 mg	Cholesterol: 8 mg
Fat: 2.7 g	Protein: 15 g	Fiber: 4 gm

White Pizza

Fennel seeds, commonly used in Italian sausage, give this crust a special flavor.

Crust	1- or 1½-pound
whole wheat, oat, or barley flour	1 cup
bread flour	1 cup
skim milk or water	¾ cup
yeast	1¼ tsp
sea salt	½ tsp
sugar	1 tsp
whole fennel seed	1 tsp
Toppings	
shredded nonfat or reduced-fat mozzarella cheese	½ cup
shredded nonfat or reduced-fat Swiss cheese	½ cup
plum tomato, thinly sliced	1 medium
grated Parmesan cheese	¼ cup
thinly sliced green onions	3 tbsp
dried crushed basil	1 tsp

Put the crust ingredients in the machine's bread pan. Use the RISE setting so that the machine will mix, knead, and allow the dough to rise. When dough has risen, turn it onto a floured surface, and roll it into a 12-inch circle. Place dough on a 12-inch pizza pan coated with cooking spray. Spread the topping ingredients over the crust in the order listed. Bake at 475° F for about 10 minutes, until the cheese is lightly browned and bubbly. This recipe makes 8 slices.

PER SERVING

Calories: 149	Sodium: 290 mg	Cholesterol: 5 mg
Fat: 1.2 g	Protein: 10 g	Fiber: 2.5 g

Sweet Stuff

THIS CHAPTER OFFERS a tempting variety of sweet treats with less fat and more fiber than most. These recipes are suitable for both 1-pound and 1½-pound machines. Use the DOUGH, RISE, or MANUAL setting to let the machine mix, knead, and allow the dough to rise once. You will then remove the dough from the machine and finish the recipe as directed.

Flour Options

Oat and *barley* flours are featured in many of these recipes. Naturally sweet and mild, these flours are perfect for pastries and sweet rolls because they impart a tender texture and reduce the need for added sugars.

Many of these recipes also include fiber-rich whole wheat flour. *White whole wheat flour* has a sweeter, lighter flavor than regular whole wheat flour and can replace regular whole wheat flour in any of these recipes. Use 1 cup plus 1 tablespoon of white whole wheat flour to substitute for 1 cup of regular whole wheat flour.

Milk Options

Milk and buttermilk are ingredients in some of these recipes. Milk adds a tender texture and rich flavor that enhances the quality of sweet breads. Soy milk and rice beverages (regular or flavored) can substitute for dairy milk in any of these recipes. Soy buttermilk can also be used instead of dairy buttermilk. To make soy buttermilk, put 1 tablespoon of vinegar in a 1-cup measure; fill to the 1-cup line with low-fat soy milk.

Sugar Options

Many of these recipes use fruit juice instead of water as a moistening agent. This reduces the need for added sugar. When a recipe does call for sugar, consider using one of the less-refined alternatives. *Sucanat,* granules of evaporated sugar-cane juice, retains many of the nutrients naturally present in sugar cane. *Date sugar* (ground dried dates) and *maple sugar* (evaporated maple syrup) are other good options. All add delicious flavor to breads; try them instead of nutrient-poor white and brown sugars.

Instead of white confectioners' sugar, try *powdered maple sugar.* Made from dried maple syrup, maple sugar is a more natural alternative to white confectioners' sugar. Realize, though, that even maple sugar is not a rich source of any nutrient. And for people with diabetes or hypoglycemia, all sugars can cause problems.

Apple-Raisin Tea Ring

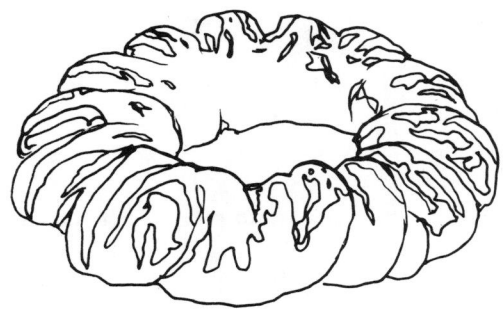

Dough	**1- or 1½-pound**
bread flour	1 cup
whole wheat flour	1 cup
oat bran	¾ cup
sugar	¼ cup
yeast	1½ tsp
sea salt	½ tsp
plain nonfat yogurt	1 cup
margarine or butter	1 tbsp
Filling	
Finely chopped apples	1¾ cups
apple juice	⅓ cup + 1 tbsp
cornstarch	1 tbsp
cinnamon	½ tsp
raisins	½ cup
Glaze	
powdered sugar	½ cup
skim milk	2 tsp
vanilla	½ tsp

Combine the dough ingredients in the machine's bread pan. Turn the machine on the RISE setting. While the dough is being prepared, make the filling. Combine 1 tablespoon of the apple juice with the cornstarch, and set it aside. Combine the remaining filling ingredients in a small pot; cover and allow it to simmer for 5 minutes. Stir in the cornstarch mixture. Cook and stir for another minute, until thick. Set the filling aside to cool.

After the dough has risen, turn it onto a lightly floured surface, and roll it into a 12 × 16-inch rectangle. Spread the filling evenly over the dough to within 1 inch of the edges. Roll up the dough from the longest side like a jelly roll, and place it seam side down on a large baking sheet coated with cooking spray. Bring the ends around to form a ring. Use scissors to snip three-fourths of the way into the ring at 1-inch intervals. Twist the slices so that the cut sides are up.

Cover and let the dough rise in a warm place for about 1 hour, until doubled in bulk. Bake at 350° F for 18 to 20 minutes, until light golden brown. Cool slightly. Combine the glaze ingredients, and drizzle the glaze over the ring while it's still warm. This recipe makes 16 slices.

PER SERVING

Calories: 132   Sodium: 88 mg   Cholesterol: 0 mg
Fat: 1.3 g   Protein: 3.6 mg   Fiber: 2.6 g

Variations

Substitute any of these fillings for the apple-raisin filling.

Maple-Walnut Filling   Combine ⅔ cup of chopped walnuts with ¼ cup of maple syrup.

Prune Filling   Combine 1 cup of chopped prunes and ¼ cup of fruit juice in a food processor. Process this filling into a thick paste.

Pineapple Filling   Combine an 8-ounce can of crushed pineapple (with juice), 2 tablespoons of sugar, and 2 tablespoons of cornstarch or arrowroot powder. Cook and stir the filling over medium heat until it's thickened. Cool to room temperature.

Quickie Fillings   Substitute 1½ cups of canned cherry, raspberry, apple, or blueberry pie filling for the apple-raisin filling.

Peach-Streusel Coffee Cake

Dough	**1- or 1½-pound**
bread flour	1 cup
oat flour or whole wheat flour	1 cup
sugar	2 tbsp
yeast	1½ tsp
sea salt	½ tsp
skim milk	¾ cup
Filling	
thinly sliced peaches	2 cups
raisins or chopped pecans	3 tbsp
sugar	2 tbsp
cornstarch	2 tsp
cinnamon	½ tsp
Streusel Topping	
brown sugar	2 tbsp
whole wheat flour	2 tbsp
quick-cooking oats	2 tbsp
cinnamon	½ tsp
maple syrup or orange-juice concentrate	1½ tbsp

Combine the dough ingredients in the machine's bread pan, and then turn machine on the RISE setting so that it will mix, knead, and allow the dough to rise once. Combine the filling ingredients and set the filling aside. Stir the topping ingredients together until moist and crumbly. Set the topping aside.

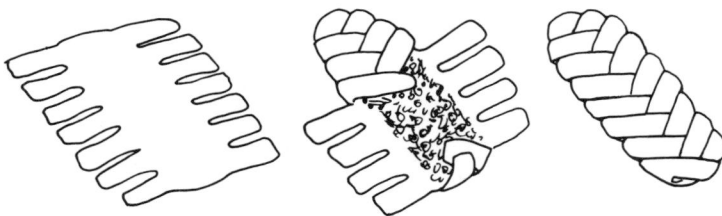

Roll the dough into a 12 × 8-inch rectangle on a lightly floured surface. Transfer the dough to a baking sheet coated with cooking spray. With a sharp knife, make

2-inch long cuts at 1-inch intervals on both of the long, 12-inch sides. Spoon the filling down the center third of the dough. Fold the strips diagonally over the filling, overlapping the strips to create a braided look.

Brush the top of the coffee cake with skim milk and spread the streusel topping over the loaf. Cover and let the dough rise in a warm place until doubled in bulk—about 45 minutes. Bake at 350° F for 25 minutes, until golden brown. Cover loosely with foil during the last 10 minutes to prevent excess browning. Serve warm. This recipe makes 12 servings.

For variety, substitute apples or pears for the peaches. To save time, a 20-ounce can of peach-pie filling may be substituted for the fresh peach filling.

PER SERVING

Calories: 134	Sodium: 116 mg	Cholesterol: 0 mg
Fat: 1.5 g	Protein: 3.4 g	Fiber: 1.9 g

Fresh Pear Kuchen

Dough	**1- or 1½-pound**
whole wheat flour	1¼ cups
bread flour	1 cup
yeast	2 tsp
sea salt	½ tsp
pear nectar	¾ cup + 2 tbsp
margarine or butter	1 tbsp
fresh pear slices	3 to 4 cups
Topping	
whole wheat flour	¼ cup + 2 tbsp
quick-cooking oats	¼ cup + 2 tbsp
brown sugar	3 tbsp
cinnamon	1⅛ tsp
nutmeg	¼ tsp
maple syrup	3 tbsp

Put the first six ingredients in the machine's bread pan and turn the machine on to RISE setting. After the dough has risen, turn it onto a lightly floured surface and roll it into a 10 × 15-inch rectangle. Place the dough on a baking sheet coated with cooking spray. Arrange the pear slices in a single layer over the dough to within ½ inch of the edges.

Combine the topping ingredients, and stir them together until they're moist and crumbly. Sprinkle the topping over the pears. Cover and let the dough rise in a warm place for about 30 minutes, until it is doubled in bulk. Bake at 350° F for 20 to 25 minutes, until light golden brown. If desired, make a glaze of ½ cup of maple sugar, ½ teaspoon of vanilla, and 2 to 3 teaspoons of pear nectar. Drizzle over the warm kuchen. This recipe makes 16 slices.

PER SERVING

Calories: 146	Sodium: 79 mg	Cholesterol: 0 mg
Fat: 1.3 g	Protein: 2.9 g	Fiber: 3.1 g

Blueberry-Cheese Foldovers

Dough	**1- or 1½-pound**
whole wheat flour	1⅓ cups
bread flour	1⅓ cups
sugar	¼ cup
yeast	1¼ tsp
sea salt	½ tsp
skim milk	¾ cup + 2 tbsp
margarine or butter	1 tbsp
Filling	
nonfat or reduced-fat cream cheese	6 ounces (¾ cup)
sugar	4 tsp
blueberry pie filling	¾ cup

Put the dough ingredients in the machine's bread pan and turn the machine on the RISE setting. When the dough has risen, turn it onto a lightly floured surface, and roll it into a 12 × 16-inch rectangle. Cut it into 12 (4-inch) squares.

Mix the cream cheese with the sugar and put 1 level tablespoon in the center of a square; top with 1 level tablespoon of blueberry filling. Fold to overlap two opposite corners. Repeat with the remaining ingredients.

Arrange the foldovers 2 inches apart on baking sheets coated with cooking spray. Cover and let them rise in a warm place until doubled in bulk—about 45 to 60 minutes. Bake at 375° F for 10 to 12 minutes, until light golden brown. This recipe makes 12 foldovers. Drizzle them with a powdered sugar glaze, if desired.

PER SERVING

Calories: 160	Sodium: 210 mg	Cholesterol: 0 mg
Fat: 1.3 g	Protein: 7 g	Fiber: 2.2 g

Hot-Cross Buns

For a real treat, use maple sugar in both the dough and the icing.

Dough	**1- or 1½-pound**
whole wheat flour	1⅔ cups
bread flour	1 cup
sugar	2 tbsp
yeast	1¼ tsp
sea salt	½ tsp
ground allspice	½ tsp
lecithin granules or vegetable oil	1 tbsp
apple juice	¾ cup + 2 tbsp
raisins	½ cup
Icing	
powered sugar	½ cup
vanilla	½ tsp
apple juice	2 tsp

Combine all the dough ingredients except the raisins in the machine's bread pan. Turn the machine on RISE setting. Add the raisins after 12 minutes or when the machine signals. After the dough has risen, shape the dough into 12 balls. Arrange the balls 2 inches apart on a baking sheet coated with cooking spray; flatten them slightly. Cover and let the dough rise in a warm place until doubled in bulk— about 45 to 60 minutes. Brush the tops with egg white glaze or skim milk. Bake at 375° F for 10 to 12 minutes, until tops are light golden brown. While warm, combine icing ingredients, and draw a cross on top of each bun with icing. This recipe makes 12 buns.

PER SERVING

Calories: 152	Sodium: 92 mg	Cholesterol: 0 mg
Fat: 1.1 g	Protein: 3.6 g	Fiber: 2.8 g

Maple-Walnut Sweet Rolls

Dough	**1- or 1½-pound**
whole wheat flour	1⅔ cups
bread flour	1 cup
sugar	2 tbsp
yeast	1¼ tsp
sea salt	½ tsp
apple juice	¾ cup + 2 tbsp
lecithin granules or vegetable oil	1 tbsp
Filling	
maple syrup	3 tbsp
chopped walnuts	¼ cup
raisins or dates	¼ cup
Icing	
maple sugar	½ cup
vanilla	½ tsp
apple juice	2 tsp

Put the dough ingredients in the machine's bread pan, and turn the machine on the RISE setting. When the dough has risen, turn it onto a lightly floured surface and roll it into a 10 × 16-inch rectangle. Spread the dough with the maple syrup and sprinkle it with the walnuts and raisins. Roll the rectangle up like a jelly roll from the long end, and cut it with a knife or a string held taut into 16 1-inch pieces.

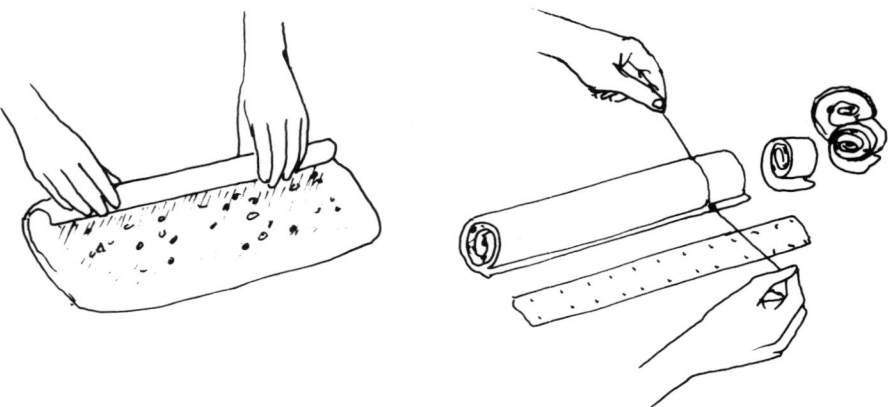

Arrange the sweet rolls 1 inch apart on a baking sheet coated with cooking spray. Cover and let them rise in a warm place until doubled in bulk—about 45 to 60 minutes. Bake at 350° F for 16 to 20 minutes, until lightly browned. Combine the icing ingredients and drizzle or spread icing over the rolls.

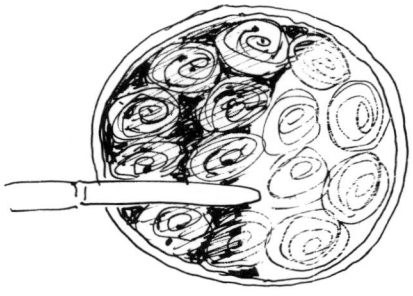

PER SERVING —————————————————————————

Calories: 128	Sodium: 69 mg	Cholesterol: 0 mg
Fat: 1.9 g	Protein: 3.1 g	Fiber: 2 g

Fruit & Nut Ring

For variety, substitute other kinds of fruits, nuts, and preserves in the filling.

Dough	1- or 1½-pound
whole-wheat flour	½ cup
oat or barley flour	½ cup
bread flour	1¼ cups
yeast	1½ tsp
sea salt	½ tsp
lecithin granules or vegetable oil	1 tbsp
applesauce	½ cup
skim milk	½ cup
Filling	
chopped dried apricots	⅓ cup
chopped walnuts	¼ cup
apricot preserves	¼ cup

Combine the dough ingredients in the machine's bread pan and turn the machine on the RISE setting. When the dough has risen, roll it into an 8 × 18-inch strip. Cut the strip into two 4 × 18-inch strips. Combine the filling ingredients and spread half along the bottom of each strip. Roll up the strip to enclose the filling and pinch it along the seams to seal.

Twist the strips around each other several times and bring the ends around to form a ring. Pinch the ends to seal. Place the ring in a 9-inch round cake pan coated with cooking spray. Cover and let it rise until doubled in bulk, about 45 minutes. Brush the top with beaten egg white or skim milk. Sprinkle 2 teaspoons of sugar over the top, if desired. Bake at 350° F for 20 to 25 minutes, until light golden brown. This recipe makes 16 slices.

PER SERVING

Calories: 106	Sodium: 72 mg	Cholesterol: 0 mg
Fat: 1.5 g	Protein: 3 g	Fiber: 1.5 g

Cranberry Coffee Ring

Dough	1- or 1½-pound
whole wheat flour	¾ cup
oat flour	½ cup
bread flour	1¼ cups
yeast	1½ tsp
sea salt	½ tsp
pear or apricot nectar	1 cup
lecithin granules or vegetable oil	1 tbsp
Filling	
finely chopped cranberries	1 cup
finely chopped dried dates	½ cup
pear or apricot nectar	¼ cup
finely chopped walnuts	2 tbsp

Put all the filling ingredients except the walnuts in a small pot. Cook and stir over medium-low heat for about 5 minutes, until very thick. Stir in the walnuts and set the filling aside to cool.

Combine the dough ingredients in machine's bread pan, and turn the machine on the RISE setting. After the dough has risen, roll it into an 10½ × 18-inch strip. Cut the strip into three 3½ × 18-inch strips. Spread one-third of the filling lengthwise along the bottom of each strip. Roll up the strips to enclose the filling and pinch them tightly along the seams to seal.

Stretch the strips to 22 inches and braid them together. Bring the ends around to form a ring. Place the coffee ring in a 9-inch round pan coated with cooking spray. Cover and let it rise until doubled in bulk—35 to 45 minutes. Brush the top with beaten egg white and sprinkle with 2 to 3 teaspoons of sugar. Bake at 350° F for about 20 minutes. This recipe makes 16 slices.

PER SERVING ————————————————————

Calories: 108	Sodium: 68 mg	Cholesterol: 0 mg
Fat: 1.4 g	Protein: 2.7 g	Fiber: 2.3 g

Poppy Seed–Almond Crescents

Dough	**1- or 1½-pound**
whole wheat flour	1 cup
brown rice flour	¼ cup
bread flour	1¼ cups
yeast	2 tsp
sea salt	½ tsp
orange juice	¾ cup
nonfat yogurt	¼ cup
margarine or butter	1 tbsp
Filling	
poppy seeds	2 tbsp
finely ground almonds	¼ cup
honey	¼ cup

Put the dough ingredients in the machine's bread pan. Turn the machine on the RISE setting. When the dough has risen, divide it into two pieces. Roll each piece into a 12-inch circle on a floured surface. Use a pizza wheel to cut each circle into eight wedges. Combine the filling ingredients and put 1 teaspoon in the center of the wide end of each wedge. Roll up each wedge from the wide end. Place the point side down on baking sheets coated with cooking spray.

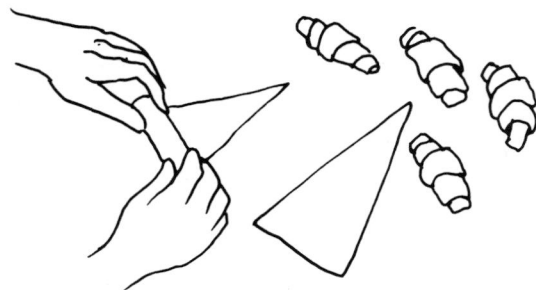

Cover and let the crescent dough rise in a warm place until doubled in bulk—about 30 minutes. Brush the tops with egg white glaze or skim milk. Bake at 375° F for 10 minutes, until lightly browned. If desired, make a glaze of ½ cup of powdered sugar, ½ teaspoon of almond extract, and 2 teaspoons of orange juice. Drizzle the glaze over the warm crescents. This recipe makes 16 crescents.

PER SERVING

Calories: 99	Sodium: 78 mg	Cholesterol: 0 mg
Fat: 2.6 g	Protein: 3 g	Fiber: 1.6 g

Sweet Potato–Cinnamon Twists

	1- or 1½-pound
whole wheat flour	2 cups
bread flour	1 cup
sugar	¼ cup
yeast	2 tsp
sea salt	½ tsp
water	¾ cup + 2 tbsp
cooked, mashed sweet potato	½ cup
raisins or chopped nuts	⅔ cup
reduced-fat margarine or light butter	2 tbsp
brown sugar	¼ cup
cinnamon	1 tsp

Put the first seven ingredients in the machine's bread pan. Turn the machine on the RISE setting so that the machine will mix, knead, and allow the dough to rise once. Add the raisins after 12 minutes or when the machine signals.

After the dough has risen, turn it onto a lightly floured surface and divide it into pieces. Roll each piece into a 12-inch square. Brush each square with half of the margarine. Combine the brown sugar and cinnamon, and sprinkle half over each square. Fold the squares in half and cut each into twelve strips from the folded end. Twist each strip twice.

Place the twists on a baking sheet coated with cooking spray. Cover them with a towel, and let them rise in a warm place until doubled in size—about 25 minutes. Bake at 375° F for 10 to 12 minutes. This recipe makes 24 twists.

PER SERVING

| Calories: 91 | Sodium: 66 mg | Cholesterol: 0 mg |
| Fat: 0.5 g | Protein: 2.2 g | Fiber: 2 g |

Index

♦ ♦ ♦